THE GIANT BOOK OF

CARD DIVINATION

130 New and Traditional Techniques

Jeanne Ruland

Illustrations by
Iris Merlino

D1521073

Sterling Publishing Co., Inc.
New York

Library of Congress Cataloging-in-Publication Data

Ruland, Jeanne.
  [Grosse Buch der Legemethoden. English]
  The giant book of card divination : 130 new and traditional techniques /
Jeanne Ruland ; illustrated by Iris Merlino.
      p. cm.
  Includes index.
  ISBN 1-4027-1804-7
  1. Fortune-telling by cards. I. Title.
  BF1878.R85 2005
  133.3'242—dc22   2004025861

TAROT cards by A.E. Waite: © 1993 by Königsfurt Publishers, D-24796 Krummwisch
By kind permission of Königsfurt Publishers.
TAROT cards A. Crowley: By kind permission of Königsfurt Publishers, C-24796 Klein
Königsförde/Krummwisch; © Ordo Templi Orientis, Austin/USA, and AG Müller,
CH-Neuhausen.
Gypsy FortuneTelling Cards. By kind permission of Fa. Piatnik & Söhne, A-Wien

Illustration: Iris Merlino
English translation: Nicole Franke and Dan Shea
Copyeditor: Bruce Macomber
Proofreader: Barbara Greenberg
Editor: Rodman Pilgrim Neumann

10 9 8 7 6 5 4 3 2 1

Published 2005 by Sterling Publishing Co., Inc.
387 Park Avenue South, New York, NY 10016
Originally published by Schirner Verlag, Darmstadt, Germany
Under the title *Das grosse Buch der Legemethoden : 130 neue
und traditionelle Legemethoden für Kartendecks aller Art*
© 2002 Schirner Verlag, Darmstadt
English translation © 2005 by Sterling Publishing Co., Inc.
Distributed in Canada by Sterling Publishing
c/o Canadian Manda Group, 165 Dufferin Street
Toronto, Ontario, Canada M6K 3H6
Distributed in Great Britain by Chrysalis Books Group PLC
The Chrysalis Building, Bramley Road, London W10 6SP, England
Distributed in Australia by Capricorn Link (Australia) Pty. Ltd.
P.O. Box 704, Windsor, NSW 2756, Australia

Sterling ISBN 1-4027-1804-7

For information about custom editions, special sales, premium and
corporate purchases, please contact Sterling Special Sales
Department at 800-805-5489 or specialsales@sterlingpub.com.

Contents

Introduction

Grant yourself space and time.
Inside of you, everything is ready.
Enter the room of eternity.
Observe the picture uncovered as you in quiet float.
It reflects a part of you that is not remote.
This part has its face within you.
This part has meaning known to be true.
Thus, behold. Let the inner door yield.
Let come forth whatever wishes to be revealed.
For you may find everything deep within you healed.

Cards: Gate Openers to, and Practical Assistance for, Today's World

Increasingly people are availing themselves of the means and methods of self-help. Laying out cards is one of those paths of inner reflection through which proper guidance can be recognized and with which the particulars of life can be analyzed. This book wishes to open the gate to this incredible tool for all people, for those beginners to the cards as well as those more advanced students. To lay out cards and to take them in as well as to receive their message is a creative and inspired path, achievable for each human being without exception if only he or she is willing to be open to it.

Today, many oracles and decks of cards are accessible that were in earlier times only exchanged and used under the strictest secrecy. Countless people already own several decks of cards, depending on their needs and preferences. When dealing with this multiplicity of cards, time and again you may be surprised to find out how inclusive and integral the range of messages can be if the cards are spread out for any aspect of existence. And this can be done with merely one or with any number of decks. Laying out cards is precisely like observing a clear lake: when it calms and rests quietly before you, a reflection becomes clear and so you come to recognize yourself.

From my many years of experience in dealing with cards from a variety of decks, I am able to say with confidence that cards, if they are accessed in a very personal manner, are speaking to us. They send us messages, give us hints, and initiate possibilities we might not easily come upon without them. If one works the cards intently, one may be able to decipher immediately the messages these cards contain.

The messages of the cards depend upon our personality and situation in life. They indicate that which has fallen upon us, that which shall fall upon us, and that which will fall upon us based upon what is happening now even when we are not aware of it. The cards can confirm a good feeling so that we can hold on to it.

The cards may also show us that which we do not wish to see. However, even in this way, we receive the opportunity to alter our present for a better future. To grant time and space to our situations in life, to observe these from the perspective that the cards show us, and then to occupy ourselves with them will bring us back onto the right path. We can once again take up the thread that often slips away in life. For in the moment in which we pause to let the cards speak, we've already begun to realign our thoughts and feelings. We are able to recognize a connection and its significance and perhaps even what we have to learn in this particular context or what we have to do next. Cards can mirror our souls if we are willing to observe them calmly and to recognize our reflection in them; furthermore, we need to be willing to embrace them and to take up their message.

With careful observation, each card has another face. Although we may all deal with the same card, it can show each of us something different, depending on context and personality. It can be very stirring to work with cards, especially when we come to realize that everything that appears in the card spread has its origin in our thoughts and in our spirit.

Cards reflect current situations in our lives; they do not cause them. Still, cards can help to change our lives. With what they show us, we can learn to assume responsibility for ourselves. When we think about the cards' message in peace and inner composure, we are able to find answers within ourselves, and thus give life a new direction.

"For hope is not in that everything turns out well but in that everything that happens has a meaning." (Source unknown)

Annotation: The term "medicine" is used in this book in the Native American Indian sense; that is, medicine is everything that helps a situation to regain balance and a feeling of harmony with the cosmos.

General Tips for Preparing to Lay Out Cards

"Whenever you are sad, disheartened or discouraged, you will find a safe cure in doing something magic." (Douglas Monroe)

- Ask yourself if you are indeed willing to look into the mirror of your soul right now. If you are merely bored or if you are simply drawing the cards as a pastime, it can happen that a card will not tell you anything at all. This is not because it does not contain any message for you, but rather because you are not ready to receive it.
- Consider laying out cards as something special, as if you were on your way to a wise prophet. Prepare for the glance into the mirror of your soul in such a way that it becomes a significant occasion for you. The better prepared and attuned you are, the more clearly and firmly the message can get through to you.
- Create a special atmosphere: for example, light a candle; play beautiful music; place something in front of you that brings you joy (a bouquet, a photograph, a figure).
- Make sure that you have quiet surroundings and that you remain undisturbed.
- Take time to think about your life.
- Try to sum up in a sentence the subject that moves you, as you would a headline or a slogan.
- Examine which card divination pattern appeals to you, which also applies to your subject, headline, or slogan.
- Choose the deck(s) of cards that you consider right for yourself.
- Put yourself in the right mood for the subject (see respective frame of mind with spreads).
- Concentrate on your heart, and ask for an answer, a message, or a hint.
- Charge the cards with your power by shuffling them or keeping them in your hand for some time.
- First, read the description of the card divination pattern before anything else. You may perhaps wish to slightly alter a question, add one, or drop one.
- When you feel ready, begin laying out the cards.
- Work step by step.
- Concentrate on the question for the respective position of the card and then draw a card. With this, you can proceed in various manners: You may draw all cards from a stack. You may draw one card, make a note of it and put it back into the stack so that all possibilities are once again open for the subsequent field. You may lay out the cards in an open or a hidden manner. You may lay out the cards from one or several decks of cards. Follow your feelings and your intuition. And realize that cards that fall out of the deck while being shuffled can also be a hint.

- Whenever you have placed down a picture of a card, it is advisable to dwell upon it for some time. To begin, calmly observe the pictures before you look up their meaning.
- When you are thus occupying yourself with a card, let it speak to you. What kind of message does the card send to you? What feelings does it provoke? Do you find them pleasant or unpleasant? What strikes you in particular about the picture? What are you thinking about when you take the card in?
- Take your time for each card as well as for the entire picture. Only then, when you have taken the card in, is it advisable to consult a book for the meaning of the card.
- Once you have deciphered the cards, it is a good idea to let them rest a moment longer and to have the effect on you continue. Sometimes taking notes can be helpful as well (e.g., with the Wheel of the Year [see p. 182] or with The Small Birthday Draw [see p. 180]), for then you can look back on them later.
- Before going to bed, think over the message of your cards once again. Often, the revelation comes overnight or within the next three days.
- If you are drawing cards as a group, you can go through the chosen card divination pattern individually or all together and then discuss the messages.
- The card divination patterns discussed in this book are envisioned in such a way that you get a comprehensive view of the situation through the cards under Companion, Master, and Joker. In this way, you also get hints about where to find support and access to deeper understanding.
- If you work intensely with a theme, your energy field will open up so that you can receive hints regarding it in everyday situations.

Further Hints and Advice

- If you lay out cards for others, create an "inhibition level" that the other person must first cross. In this way, you can make sure that your "client" truly wishes to look at the cards. This inhibition level may be a small sum of money, a particularly arranged corner that needs to be entered, or the like.
- Despite its playful character, laying out cards can trigger far-reaching processes. Therefore, it is advisable that you lay out a complete pattern of a card in order to see everything. If you notice that a crisis is about to take place, try to prepare your client for it so that he or she seeks support from someone with greater knowledge of the subject. In any given situation, laying out cards can be door opener, assistance, or catalyst; however, it is not a substitute for therapy and medical treatment.

The Arrangement of the Book

The following points explain the presentation scheme, detailing how the card divination patterns that are introduced are set up.

Object of This Card Divination   Here, the purpose of each of the card divination patterns is explained.

Getting into the Right Mood   This section introduces the subject, possible questions, as well as hints to get attuned to the theme.

Card Divination Pattern   A step-by-step explanation of the card divination pattern with illustration.

The Meaning of Card Symbols in the Card Divination Patterns

General

The foundation: For this you may use the cards from a deck of your choice. Those card decks that allow for various meanings and possibilities of messages, such as tarot cards are most recommended.

Illustration: *General* Card

Base

The elemental power: Here, you may employ all decks of cards listed in the chart on pages 15-16, under Base Cards. Most recommended are those decks in which the four elements or basic statements regarding life situations are grasped, such as the Lesser Arcana within the tarot cards.

Illustration: *Base* Card

Companion

The support: For this, you may use all card decks listed in the chart on pages 15-16 under Companion. Most recommended are those decks of cards with which you feel supported, fortified, and filled with strength.

Illustration: *Companion* Card

Master

The apprenticeship: All card decks belonging to this are listed in the chart on pages 15-16 under Master. Most recommended are those decks that have a centrally far-reaching and higher message. Here, you may open books of wisdom and theological sermons of spiritual teachers as well, such as the Bible.

Illustration: *Master* Card

Joker

The surprise: Here you may employ all decks of cards that are listed in the chart on pages 15-16 as Joker Card Decks. Most recommended are those decks whose cards may bring about an unpredictable initial stage but round off and complete the entire message of those cards drawn so far, such as healing cards, Bach flower cards, color cards, etc.

Illustration: *Joker* Card

Hint/Advice

At this point, you will find an addition at the end of each card divination pattern. Here, possibilities of variation for the introduced spreads may be listed; or you may find hints for which spread might be additionally employed as well as tips for the subject in question.

General Advice for Using Card Divination Patterns

The card divination patterns in this book are provided with a maximum of five symbols corresponding with the five types of cards (General, Base, Companion, Master, and Joker). Depending on which of these types of cards appear in the card divination pattern introduced, that many card decks can be used in it and can be laid out in the sequence stated.

You may modify each spread according to your feeling; for example by laying out all questions with one single card deck. Another possibility is to consult another deck only for Companions and Masters or by only taking in another deck for Master and Joker respectively; this is entirely up to you. Choose the cards that appeal to you and are important to you. Here are a few more suggestions:

- If you are using a tarot deck, it can be divided as follows: Base-The Lesser Arcana; Companion-The Court Cards; Master/Joker- The Greater Arcana.
- You can also work with two decks; for example, you may use a basic deck such as tarot for all fields and, for the Companion fields, for example, use only an angel card set, or, for the Joker fields, an additional card from another deck.
- For another adaptation you may first lay out a general deck, such as tarot, onto all fields and then proceed by laying out a second round with the given decks according to the described scheme. By doing this, you receive additional information and greater explanation of the individual fields.
- You may also work with two to three tarot decks by laying out two or three rounds precisely with another deck of cards each time.
- Another variant is to subdivide all decks of cards into the five stated categories (General, Base, Companion, Master, and Joker) and then lay them out. If the card divination pattern mentions only one Companion, but you have three Companion decks (e.g., three different angel sets), you may draw three Companion cards for the subject.
- If you wish to lay out cards with several people, each person may bring a deck of cards. These cards then become the foundation for the chosen card divination pattern(s). First, divide the card decks that were brought along into five categories. Introduce these sets of cards to one another. In cases where there are three decks among them that could be considered Companion, or Master, or Joker, it is recommended that you also use them. In this way, each person in the group can contribute something and thus the group energy is increased.

Whatever way you finally lay out the cards depends on your personal card stockpile and your feelings. Before you lay out the cards, ask yourself each time: With which cards do I want to work in this card divination pattern? Examine which decks feel good and right for the subject at hand. The most important principle is that the spread feels right to you and that a message is conveyed to you.

Criteria Helpful in Finding the Right Card Decks

- Listen to your feelings.
- What card decks do you have at hand?
- If you want to buy a deck of cards, do so but take your time. Observe the pictures. Read through the text. Ask yourself: Does it appeal to you? Does it open up your heart? Are you looking forward to it? Does it help you?
- Do you want to work with only one or with several decks?
- Which card decks do you wish to consult now, at this very moment?
- Which cards give you strength? Which cards are for you?
- What is your theme?
- What is your goal—an encompassing view or a short answer? Are you capable of phrasing your theme in such a way that it can be answered by "yes" or "no"; or does it require an extensive explanation and longer exposition?
- Which cards have an especially strong message and validity?
- You may choose aids in order to make the right choice; for example, you may work with a pendulum and the following pendulum charts.

Overall View of Various Card Decks and Possible Classifications

Basically, any deck of cards can be used for answering each question. However, you should pay attention to the existence—in terms of your being—of a relationship between question/subject and deck. The cards should be expressive of you and speak to you.

In the following chart you will find an overall view of various card decks and possible classifications for the General, Base, Companion, Master, and Joker categories. This is good for orientation and might clarify through classifying. However, it is ultimately up to you to divide the decks that you have at home according to your own judgment and feeling and then assign them.

Most of the card decks are suitable for several categories. However, it is advisable to use each one in only one or two categories. If the cards of one are classified, for example, as Master, it is useful to view them as something special and higher and to use them in a card divination pattern only once.

In this respect, tarot cards are exceptional since they contain all possibilities. In any case, they can serve as a base that can be supplemented with other card decks if desired. Tarot cards are expressive in each category, and so there are numerous possibilities of variation. Each spread can be laid entirely with tarot cards. Other card decks may be supplementally consulted in the manner described with the respective card divination patterns.

In addition, tarot cards may be divided among themselves once more: into the Greater Arcana, the Lesser Arcana, and the Court Cards. The Greater Arcana are 22 main cards from 0, "The Fool," to 22, "The World." The Lesser Arcana consist of four symbols/elements: The Suit of Cups, The Suit of Swords, The Suit of Wands, and The Suit of Pentacles, each from

Ace up to 10. The Court Cards are those that are assigned to the four symbols; however, they have precedence over the Lesser Arcana. Each symbol has its own "royal household": King/Prince, Queen, Knight, Jack/Page/Princess (the descriptions differ with various decks). Suggestions for division of the Greater Arcana, the Lesser Arcana and the Court Cards can be found in the chart.

This chart does not claim to be complete.

Sets of Cards from A to Z	General	Basic	Companion	Master	Joker
Activity Set, Female Wisdom	X	X	X	X	X
Angel Cards, in general			X		X
Angel Game			X		
Archangel Cards			X		X
Aromatherapy Cards			X		X
AstroCards			X		X
Astro-Dice Oracle					X
Astrology Cards, general	X	X	X	X	X
Astrology of Fate			X		X
Aura Soma Set			X		X
Bach Flower Cards			X		X
Buddha Cards			X	X	X
Cards of Fire			X	X	X
Cards of Power			X		X
Chakra Cards, in general		X	X	X	X
Chakra Energy Cards		X	X		X
Color Cards, in general		X	X		X
Color Diagnosis Cards		X	X		X
Court Cards in Tarot, in general		X	X		
Curative Colors		X	X		X
Delphi Oracle		X	X		X
Dragon Oracle				X	X
Dual Soul Oracle					X
Egyptian Oracle			X		X
Element Cards, in general		X			
Enneagram					X
Faerie Oracle			X		X

Sets of Cards from A to Z	General	Basic	Companion	Master	Joker
Feng Shui					X
Flower Speaks Deck			X		X
Goddesses Whispering			X	X	X
Greater Arcana in Tarot, in general			X	X	X
Heart Cards			X		X
I Ching for Magic Witches				X	X
I Ching, in general				X	X
I Ching of Love				X	X
Inspiration Cards; the Gizeh Oracle				X	X
In the Kingdom of Nature Spirits		X	X		X
Kabbala Oracle		X		X	X
Karma Cards		X			X
Keys to the Heavens and Star Gates				X	X
Kipper—Prophetic Cards	X	X	X	X	X
Lesser Arcana in Tarot, in general	X	X			
Listen to Your Body		X			X
Love Whispering					X
Medicinal Herb Cards		X	X		X
Medicinal Plants—Color Cards		X	X		X
Presence of the Masters				X	X
Realization Cards				X	X
Soul Motion		X			X
Transcending Duality—Zen Koans			X	X	X

Number of Card Decks

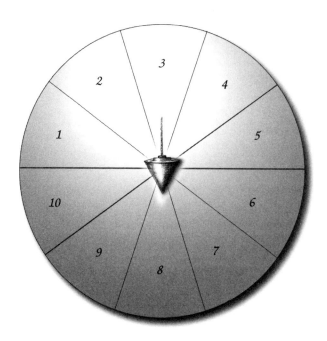

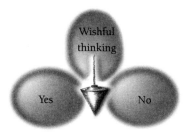

From this pendulum chart and with the help of a pendulum, you can find out how many card decks you need for the chosen card divination pattern.

Base Cards

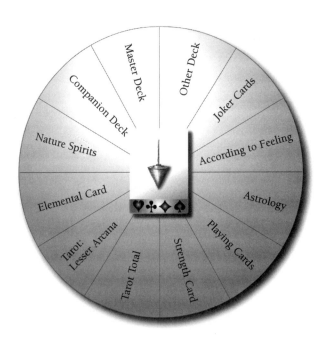

From this pendulum chart and with the help of a pendulum, you can find out which card decks are suitable as *Base Cards* for the chosen card divination pattern.

General Cards

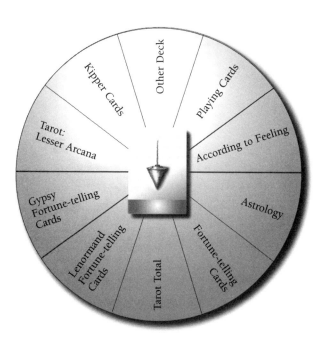

Kipper Cards

Other Deck

Playing Cards

Tarot: Lesser Arcana

According to Feeling

Gypsy Fortune-telling Cards

Astrology

Lenormand Fortune-telling Cards

Tarot Total

Fortune-telling Cards

Wishful thinking

Yes

No

From this pendulum chart and with the help of a pendulum, you can find out which card decks are suitable as *General Cards* for the chosen card divination pattern.

Pendulum Chart

Companion Cards

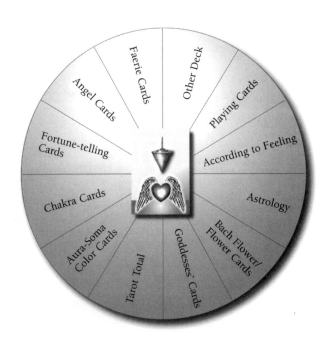

- Faerie Cards
- Other Deck
- Angel Cards
- Playing Cards
- Fortune-telling Cards
- According to Feeling
- Chakra Cards
- Astrology
- Aura-Soma Color Cards
- Bach Flower/Flower Cards
- Tarot Total
- Goddesses' Cards

- Wishful thinking
- Yes
- No

From this pendulum chart and with the help of a pendulum, you can find out which card decks are suitable as *Companion Cards* for the chosen card divination pattern.

Master Cards

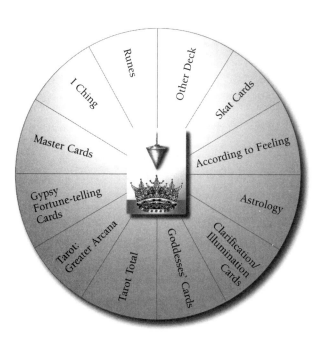

From this pendulum chart and with the help of a pendulum, you can find out which card decks are suitable as *Master Cards* for the chosen card divination pattern.

Joker Cards

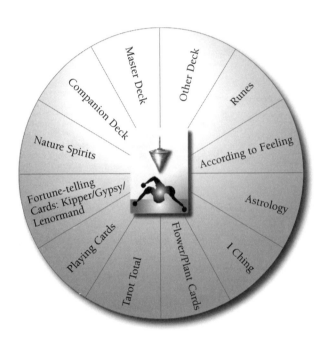

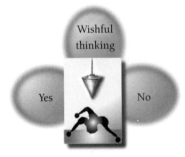

From this pendulum chart and with the help of a pendulum, you can find out which card decks are suitable as Joker Cards for the chosen card divination pattern.

Card Divination
Patterns

The Celtic Cross

General

Object of This Card Divination

This card divination pattern is generally popular for questioning the oracle. It can be employed for all the themes of our everyday lives.

Getting into the Right Mood

The Celtic Cross is one of the most popular and one of the oldest card divination patterns. It is named after the figure formed by the first six cards. In your own manner, attune yourself to the oracle. Concentrate on your current situation in life. What questions occupy you at the moment? For which questions do you seek an answer? The more precisely your questions are formulated and the more clearly envisioned your situation, the more the cards will reveal to you concerning your current situation in life.

Base

Card Divination Pattern

General (Base)

1. The basic theme/the central statement/that which it is all about
2. Hindering/fostering influences that influence the basic theme
3. The root/the base/the cause of the current situation
4. The recent past/that which just happened
5. Possible result
6. Future influences/that which is just beginning
7. What I contribute to the situation
8. What the outside world contributes to the situation
9. Hopes or fears
10. Result/key/that which will continue to occupy me for some time

Companion (Support)

11. That which accompanies and supports me
12. That which assists me in crisis situations

Master (Apprenticeship)

13. The message of this time

Joker (Surprise)

14. That which helps and heals me
15. The reserve/that which is at my disposal and did not come to my mind before

Tip/Advice

As with other popular card divination patterns, you may add additional cards for Companion, Master, and Joker cards in order to round off the picture and to develop an integral view. We are not only passive in a situation, but we can also create it and learn from it. It is part of our process of development.

Joker

Gypsy Fortune-telling

General

Object of This Card Divination
This card divination pattern is a fortune-telling method with which you may explore what the future has in store for you, drawing upon your current situation.

Getting into the Right Mood
Light a candle and concentrate on your present circumstances. Choose 1 to 3 card decks. Concentrate on each question in turn, and draw your cards with great care.

Base

Card Divination Pattern
General (Foundation)
   1. What is now?
   2. What covers me (what lies above me)?
   3. What terrifies me?
   4. What drives me?
   5. What remains for me?
   6. What the near future holds for me?
   7. What forces me to stay grounded?

Base (Elemental power)
   8. The natural strength I can tap into (where my strength lies)

Companion

Companion (Support)
   9. That which accompanies me in the time of need
   10. That which guides me by a beloved hand

Master (Apprenticeship)
   11. That which the cosmos promises me

Joker (Surprise)
   12. That which sparks the inner light

Master

Tip/Advice
For this card divination pattern, special card decks that are specifically used as an oracle are suitable, e.g., Lenormand Fortune-telling Cards, Gypsy Fortune-telling Cards, Kipper Fortune-telling Cards, etc. Of course, though, you may also use any other card deck.

Joker

The Star Oracle

General

Object of This Card Divination

The Star Oracle sets the gaze free into the realm of dreams, that space between worlds and beyond time.

Getting into the Right Mood

"Oh, you stars high above, tell me where the path leads. On my journey you look with love, from the higher point of view, for your cosmic light accompanies and guides me, too. Thus, I turn my gaze into the distance upon you beautiful stars and ask. For I know you are pleased to lead me on my task."

Base

The stars have been guiding people since the world began. They are our orientation and they show us guidelines and laws. Their position relative to one another describes the play of forces corresponding to the happenings on earth; for just as it is on a large scale, so it is on a small scale and vice versa. Gaze upon the night sky. Let yourself be inspired by the brilliance of the stars. Imagine what forces currently prevail in your life. To do this, close your eyes and attune yourself to the eternity of the cosmos. Then choose your cards, start to lay them out and see what reveals itself to you.

Companion

Card Divination Pattern

General (Foundation)

1. The starlight
2. One's inner perception
3. That which helps me or blocks me
4. That which is secretly guiding me now
5. That which touches me deeply
6. That which subtly prompts me
7. That which I do not wish to see
8. That which the star is telling me now

Master

Companion (Support)

9. Cosmic escort

Master (Apprenticeship)

10. The higher meaning of this time

Joker (Surprise)

11. The gift of eternity

Joker

Tip/Advice

Dwell upon the drawn cards for quite some time until you have grasped the message deep inside you. If the feeling strikes you, you may observe the result of The Star Oracle with the card divination pattern The Principle of Correspondence [see p. 258].

The Interpretation of Dreams

General

Object of This Card Divination
This card divination pattern helps to examine the message of a dream in greater detail and perhaps even decode it.

Getting into the Right Mood

> *"In the strange, lighthearted manner of our soul, a dream teaches us to penetrate into each object and to immediately transform ourselves into it."*
>
> (Novalis, German poet, 1772–1801)

Base

A dream is an encoded message from our soul. If we do not open this nocturnal missive, we cannot receive the messages that come from our very depths to us. There are many kinds of dreams: dreams that merely process the day's happenings and reflect them; these dreams take place if we do not review our day before going to sleep. Then there are dreams with a deep message; here, we learn of the teachings and guidance from higher worlds. These are the dreams in which we travel and are active. If we dwell within these dreams more intensely, we will notice some fine differences with time. We may even gradually learn to enter a dream and to consciously guide it in a certain direction. This dream level offers many pos-

Companion

sibilities.

Here are some questions for attuning yourself: Which dream do you wish to decipher? What are the objects that appeared in the dream (N.B.: Everything has a meaning here: shape, color, movement.)? Which feelings did the dream raise within you? What thoughts did the dream trigger? What emotional effect does the dream have on you? With which theme in life could the dream be connected? Write down your dream and compose questions concerning it. Choose your cards, and then begin laying them out.

Card Divination Pattern

Master

General (Foundation)
>   1. Central theme: The dream
>   2. The dream's message
>   3. Hidden message of the dream
>   4. What the dream relates to
>   5. How the message of the dream should be put into practice

Base (Elemental power)
>   6. Which of the elements stand in relation to the dream

Companion (Support)
>   7. The force that helps me to understand the dream

Master (Apprenticeship)
>   8. Under which star does the dream stand?

Joker

Joker (Surprise)
>   9. What supports the message of the dream now?

Tip/Advice

Let the cards take effect for some time. Look at them once more before going to bed, and ask to be allowed to decipher the message in greater detail. Sometimes, it takes a while until the message of the cards develops itself into a theme.

The High Priestess
A Look into the Mirror

General

Object of This Card Divination
With the help of this card divination pattern, you can gaze into the inner mirror to see how things stand and where the journey leads.

Getting into the Right Mood

Base

In earlier times, people sought advice from the High Priestess on everyday occasions and especially on special occasions to see how things stand, what needs to be done or refrained from, or whether the time is favorable for action. The High Priestess grants sight into one's inner mirror.

Before you begin laying out the cards, take a moment to attune yourself to the High Priestess. Close your eyes and embrace your inner peace. Assume a receptive position. When you feel ready, choose your cards and begin to lay them out.

Card Divination Pattern

General (Foundation)

Companion

1. Central theme
2. Intensifying/disturbing aspect of the theme
3. Main influence
4. Increasing influence
5. Decreasing influence
6. Dark side of the moon
7. Illuminated side of the moon
8. Where the journey leads: the look in the mirror

Companion (Support)

9. What escorts the journey

Master (Apprenticeship)

Master

10. The highlight of the journey

Joker (Surprise)

11. The secret of the High Priestess (what she will send with you on the journey)

Tip/Advice

Joker

Meditate upon the drawn cards for some time until the message clearly takes shape. If things become confusing, you can always go back to the cards before going to bed and ask for an answer. Sometimes this answer comes in the form of a dream. Often the strength of the moon, the sign under which the High Priestess stands, acts via the dream level: if you wish to find still deeper access to the message of the High Priestess, you can, for example, continue working with the card divination patterns in the chapter Hermetic Principles [see pp. 256–269].

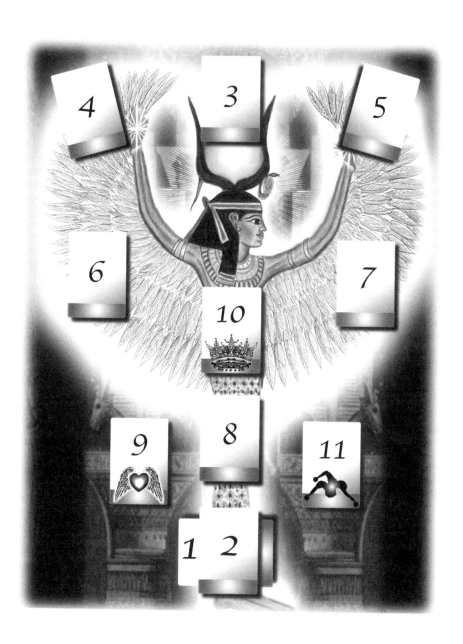

The Seven Parables

General

Object of This Card Divination
This card divination pattern will help you to assess ventures of all kinds.

Getting into the Right Mood
Each of the seven cards in this card divination pattern relates a parable that deals with the major questions one faces in this life. These short didactic dramas will give you information about your present circumstances and what is next on the program.

Base

Here are some questions for attuning yourself: If you were to tell the story of your life right now, what kind of story would it be: a funny one, a sad one, a tragic one, a serious one, a ceremonial one, a reverent one, or a boring story? Take your time, and think about your current situation in life. Does the story that you are bringing to paper appeal to you? If not, what can you change about it? What are you contributing to the story? Attune yourself to your situation in life in your own way, choose your cards, and then begin laying them out. Let each card tell you a little story in complement to your larger one.

Card Divination Pattern

General (Foundation)

Companion

1. Past: What is about to come to an end
2. Present: The current moment
3. Future: That which is just beginning
4. What is to be done now
5. The helpful or disturbing energy from the outside
6. Hopes or fears on the inside
7. Result/outcome/key: That which will occupy you awhile longer

Base (Elemental power)

8. The natural force that acts in your life

Companion (Support)

Master

9. That which gives you strength and hope in all situations

Master (Apprenticeship)

10. The star under which this phase is currently standing

Joker (Surprise)

11. The secret reserve: What is still at your disposal

Joker

The Small Fork
A Small Decision: Yes or No?

General

Object of This Card Divination
This method is applicable to all areas in which we face a decision. Here, you can sift through your options so that you can make a clear decision afterward.

Getting into the Right Mood

Base

Before you begin laying out your cards, determine your theme. You have chosen your own path in this matter up to this time and have now reached a point where the road divides. You do not wish to go back; therefore, you will have to decide for one or the other options that lie ahead of you. If you choose one way, you will not be able to go the other one. The one way means "yes," the other one means "no." Which way should you choose? Which way will lead you to which goal? Which advantages and disadvantages does one path have? And which advantages and disadvantages does the other possess? Consider how things are currently standing. Formulate a question to your theme that can be answered with yes or no, and then begin laying out the cards.

Card Divination Pattern

Companion

General (Foundation)
1. The theme
2. Yes
3. No
4. Yes. What needs to be observed/considered?
5. What happens if I do it?
6. How does it turn out?
7. No. What needs to be observed/considered?
8. What happens if I am not going to do it?
9. How does it turn out?

Companion (Support)
10. Which force accompanies me if I say yes?
11. Which force accompanies me if I say no?

Master

Master (Apprenticeship)
12 What is the core message with "yes"?
13. What is the core message with "no"?

Joker (Surprise)
14. Which secret is revealed to me if I say yes?
15. Which secret is revealed to me if I say no?

Joker

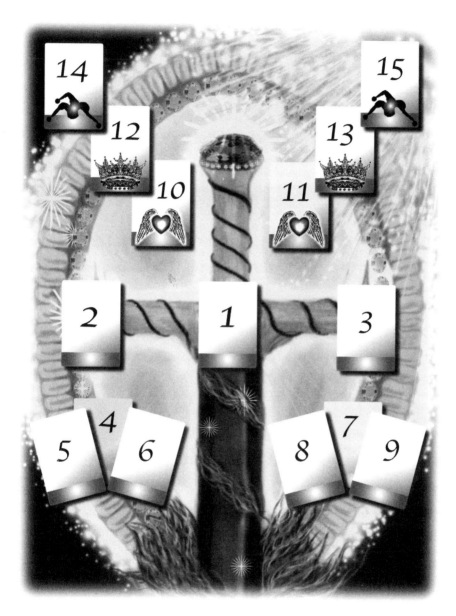

Tip/Advice

If you have already found an answer for yourself with cards 1 to 3, the card divination is complete. If, however, you wish to know more details, then it is good to work on all of the questions.

General

The Great Fork

A Big Decision: Which Direction Should I Take?

Object of This Card Divination

This card divination pattern can offer help with major decisions. Here, you can mentally play through several options before you will have to make your choice and head in one direction.

Getting into the Right Mood

Base

You have gone one way. This way has become wider and wider. Then you reach a fork in the road, and with it, with many possibilities. You may stay on the path you have been taking up to this point. You may slightly deviate toward the left or right. You can, however, head in an entirely new direction. The experiences you have gained while taking the old path will help you.

Before you begin laying out the cards, concentrate on your theme. Which way have you been taking all the time? What have you learned by doing so? What do you want to do next? What is your wish? What is your goal? What are your hopes? What are your fears? What are your options? You may create a pattern with one to four decks.

Companion

Card Divination Pattern

General (Foundation)

  1. Central theme: Starting point/base
  2. That which is hidden
  3. On the one hand: What needs to be observed?
  4. On the other hand: What needs to be observed?
  5. Past: What do I take with me from the path that lies behind me?
  6. My strength: What ability have I already developed?

Master

  7. Self-assessment
  8. Assessment of others

Companion (Support)

  9. Which force has been accompanying me so far?

General (Foundation)

  10. Has the time come to consider new possibilities?

Joker (Surprise)

  11. What does the oracle say to that?

Joker

If cards 9 and 10 say no, draw another card in regards to the question: Why not? By doing so, the card divination pattern has been completed for you at this point, and you should perhaps repeat it at another point in time.

If cards 9 and 10 say yes, then lay out some cards for the possibilities that you are facing and four other cards at any one time for each subsequent possibility:

General (*Foundation*)

12. Possibility: What is going to happen if I stay on this path?
13. On the one hand
14. On the other hand

Companion (*Support*) *and/or* **Master** (*Apprenticeship*)

15. Which force accompanies me and aids me along the way?

Joker (*Surprise*)

16. The oracle of the future: How does it end?

Apply steps 12 through 16 for each of your options. If you still do not notice any particular possibilities, you may also check the following options (if you wish, you may draw an additional Companion card for each):

1st possibility: What happens if I deviate only slightly from the path?

2nd possibility: What happens if I head into a completely new direction?

3rd possibility: What happens if I do not undertake anything and head in neither the one or the other direction?

4th possibility: What happens if I combine the old path with a new direction?

Tip/Advice

From the four above-mentioned possibilities, you may choose—and lay out—only those that are possible for you.

The Way Out

General

Object of This Card Divination

This card divination pattern will help you to find a way out, should you find yourself stuck in a dead-end situation.

Getting into the Right Mood

You are stuck in a dead-end street. Your thoughts circle incessantly around one theme only, and you can find neither solution nor way out. Take a few minutes to determine the theme of your dead-end street; this is best done as an action (e.g., should I take on the new job, devote myself to a new partner, establish a family?). What is your problem? What are your thoughts regarding the subject? When did the difficulties start? What is your wish? What are your anxieties and hopes?

Base

After you have become attuned for some time to the paralyzing situation, begin laying out your cards.

Card Divination Pattern

General (Foundation)

1. My thoughts circle around this topic
2. What happens if I go for it?
3. The feeling that will be triggered within me if I go for it
4. The manner in which my environment perceives me if I go for it
5. What happens if I do not go for it?
6. The feeling that will be triggered within me if I do not go for it
7. The manner in which my environment perceives me if I do not go for it
8. What prevents me?
9. What encourages me?
10. What helps me out of this situation?

Companion

Companion (Support)

11. Which force accompanies me if I decide to go for it?
12. Which force accompanies me if I do not decide to go for it?

Master (Apprenticeship)

13. Under this star, under this guidance my theme stands

Joker (Surprise)

14. What is helping me at this moment and what is healing me?

Master

Tip/Advice

Joker

If something occupies an inordinate amount of your time, take a break from it. Surrender your problem to higher powers (e.g., to the angels), and let them handle the situation; let your mind rest and your soul relax. Take some time for yourself, and do something that gives you pleasure. In this way, you will give other forces the opportunity to work for you. Sometimes, you receive the first signs very soon after and the way out comes about all by itself.

The Eisenhower Method

General

Object of This Card Divination

This card divination pattern will help you create an overview concerning your situation in life and recognize an order therein.

Getting into the Right Mood

Dwight D. Eisenhower (1890–1969) was first a general and then the 34th president of the United States. He developed his very own methods to see, grasp, and handle things quickly, and, in particular here, crisis situations. The Eisenhower Method was considered the work secret of many US presidents for a long time. However, it has become generally known and is used in many areas for maintaining the flow of life. It works like this:

Base

Divide the areas in your life into four fields:

Field 1: This field contains those things that should be eliminated from your life, those things that hinder and block you or take energy from you on all levels. What can I sort out in my life?

Field 2: This field contains everything that does not have to be taken care of by you necessarily, but could also be handled by others who might assume some of the responsibility. What tasks do not have to necessarily be taken care of by you? What can you pass on, forward to someone else? What tasks can colleagues, family members, or services take off your shoulders?

Companion

Field 3: This field contains everything that has to be done in the very near future, those things that are urgent and must be handled only by you. It is also the field that contains everything that means a lot to you and for you.

Field 4: Everything that you can do immediately is stored here as you occupy yourself with your circumstances, your job, and your problems. It also reveals that which is still at your disposal and had not been thought of up to this point.

Master

Before you begin laying out your cards, divide the table in front of you in the above-mentioned four fields. Take some time and think about your situation in life. What is currently occupying your mind? What is your question? Let everything that recently happened and is occupying your mind come to the surface. Then think about what you would put in which field. You may also take some quick notes. As soon as you have acquired a feeling for your situation of life, begin laying out your cards according to the Eisenhower Method.

Joker

Card Divination Pattern

General (Foundation)

You may draw one or two cards per field; do what feels right to you.

1. *Field 1:* What should I let go of? What has become superfluous?
2. *Field 2:* What can be handed over? What may I delegate to others?
3. *Field 3:* What can be taken care of only by me? What should I take care of in the very near future?
4. *Field 4:* What can I do in this very moment? What needs to be done now?

Base *(Elemental power)*

5. Which power predominates at the moment?

Companion *(Support)*

6. What is by my side? What supports me right now?

Master *(Apprenticeship)*

7. What opportunity for growth does this situation, this task, or this problem bring with it?

Joker *(Surprise)*

8. What have I not thought of yet? What is still at my disposal in this situation?

Tip/Advice

You may also want to work with other card divination patterns that deal specifically with your subject.

Clarifying Ambiguous Cards

General

Object of This Card Divination

Here, you may examine a distant or inaccessible card more thoroughly in order to reach a closer meaning.

Getting into the Right Mood

Place the card that you wish to examine more closely in the middle on the field "Card about which I wish to learn more." Think once again about the context in which you have drawn it. What was your question? On which spot did it lie in the previously laid spread? What was the subject? What is the statement of the card? What is not accessible to you? Determine for yourself once again the subject and the circumstances. Then start.

Base

Card Divination Pattern

General (Foundation)
1. The blind spot: What I do not wish to see
2. The second face of this card: further meanings of this card
3. The tip: What the card wishes to hint at; what it wants to tell me

Companion (Support)
4. Power: That which gives me strength
5. Special attention: The force I am supposed to activate/recognize

Companion

Tip/Advice

If the card still not does tell you anything, let what you have just drawn rest for some time and dwell upon it for at least three days. Sometimes, there is an inner resistance that does not allow the message to come immediately to the surface. You may also wish to work with the Blind Spot card divination pattern [see p. 134].

Master

Joker

Friendship/Comradeship

General

Object of This Card Divination
With this card, you may closely examine your relationships with other people.

Getting into the Right Mood
Friendship is one of the most wonderful things that exist: to rely on the other person; to have someone who stands by our side even in difficult times; to go with somebody through thick and thin; to joke around together; to have fun together; to share secrets with one another and not to give anything away; to exchange things; to stand by each other and yet let the other go his or her way; to gather experiences together and to share them. Shared sorrows are halved. A friend is someone upon whom we can always rely. Most people know the feeling of friendship. No matter what happens, life will be dealt with together. Sometimes, one person might lose touch with the other for some time, but a reunion is always possible. People share memories about a time spent together.

Base

Here are some questions for attuning yourself: Have you experienced the feeling of friendship? How important is friendship for you and how highly would your rate it? What connects you to your friends? In your opinion, what is so special about friendships? Attune yourself to the theme. You may lay out this card divination pattern alone, with one friend, or with several. If you lay out the cards as a group, you may want to draw alternately.

Companion

Card Divination Pattern
General (Foundation)
1. Central theme/friendship/our friendship
2. What connects us
3. What secretly connects us
4. What we appreciate most about our friendship
5. What we give to one another
6. Where we hinder or nurture ourselves
7. The danger of our friendship
8. The task of our friendship
9. The gift of our friendship
10. The chance of development in our friendship
11. The future of our friendship

Master

Base (Elemental Power)
12. Which natural power needs to be particularly observed in our relationship

Companion (Support)
13. The power that accompanies our friendship
14. The power that helps our friendship and protects it in difficult situations

Joker

Master *(Apprenticeship)*

    15. The star under which our friendship stands

Joker *(Surprise)*

    16. What the oracle has to say about our friendship

    17. The special gift of our friendship

    18. What always helps our friendship and heals it

The Ideal Partner

The Soul Mate

General

Object of This Card Divination

This card divination pattern helps you to envision the ideal partner, the soul mate, and your idea of partnership in general.

Getting into the Right Mood

Base

Our visionary power gives us courage for creativity, courage for change, and courage to follow new ways. When we occupy ourselves with our partner/ideal partner/soul mate, we begin to send our signals out into the world. By doing so, the first steps have been taken to invite our ideal partner, our soul mate into our world. We begin to open the inner door for a partnership, to make room inside of us for the partnership, for the person who is our second half and with whom we can build a circle of power.

Here are some questions for attuning yourself: What are your ideas of a partner, of a relationship? What do you wish for? What are you willing to give? How do you imagine a relationship? Which role do you play, and which role does your partner play? Attune yourself to the theme and then begin laying out your cards.

Companion

Card Divination Pattern

General (Foundation)

    1. My ideal partner/my soul mate

    2. Me

    3. My wish for the relationship

    4. My hidden theme of a relationship

    5. How can we meet?

    6. What connects us?

    7. What separates us?

    8. What obstacles might we encounter on our path?

    9. How will I recognize my ideal partner?

    10. What tasks are we supposed to fulfill together?

Base (Elemental power)

    11. What natural force needs to be observed in particular?

Companion (Support)

    12. Which force helps me to recognize my ideal partner?

    13. Which force supports or accompanies the encounter?

Master (Apprenticeship)

    14. Under which star does our encounter stand?

Joker (Surprise)

    15. What opens the door now?

Master

Joker

Tip/Advice

In order to deepen the subject, you may want to work with these card divination patterns: The Inner Woman [see p. 74], The Inner Man [see p. 76], The Inner Couple [see p. 78] for as the inside goes, so does the outside. The spreads The Principle of Correspondence [see p. 258] and The Principle of Gender [see p. 268] are also good possibilities to complement your work.

The Karmic Connection

General

Object of This Card Divination

With this card divination pattern, one can examine a partnership/relationship more thoroughly and so come to understand it better.

Getting into the Right Mood

Base

By the phrase "karmic connection" one understands a fateful connection; a connection from an earlier time, from an earlier life. This is a connection that was desired by fate so that things that happened some time in the past could and can be continued, pursued or worked on, forgiven, taken care of, and/or dissolved. A person can recognize a karmic connection in that the other individual is familiar although he or she has possibly never been seen before; that there is an immediate liking on both sides; that the feelings for the other person are unusually impetuous and run very deep. Everything develops into a direction that almost seems foreordained and so leaves no room for choice. Events become independent, and no one exerts any discernable influence over them. It feels like a connection from another world and from another life that has existed for a long time. If these are the feelings that you are experiencing in a relationship, then you are most certainly dealing with a

Companion

karmic connection.

Now you can examine what you need to resolve: Which feelings prevail in this relationship? What is the theme that appears time and again and what is the pattern that repeats itself even in different variations? What catchphrase would you use to describe the connection, and what title would you give it? What historical time do you both love? What are the likings or aversions that you have in common? What connects you deeply? Attune yourself to the theme and then begin laying out the cards.

Card Divination Pattern

Master

General (Foundation)

1. Our relationship/our union
2. My power of fate/Where do I come from?
3. My partner's power of fate/Where does my partner come from?
4. From where do we know each other?
5. What has connected each other earlier (in an earlier life)? What was our task?
6. What connects us today? What is our task today?
7. What do I mean to my partner?
8. What does my partner mean to me?

Joker

9. What needs to be recovered/worked on/developed further?
10. Where does our union lead us?
11. What is the chance of growth within our current union?

Base *(Elemental Power)*

12. What natural force do we need to particularly observe in our relationship?

Companion *(Support)*

13. What comes to aid our union from the spiritual world?

14. Which force accompanies our union?

Master *(Apprenticeship)*

15. Under which star does our union stand?

16. Which cosmic power assists us in further developing/redeeming our relationship?

Joker *(Surprise)*

17. What helps us and heals our relationship?

18. What helps us to develop, pursue/redeem our karmic affair?

Tip/Advice

If you wish to continue working on this subject, you can do so with the Visiting the Karmic Council spread [see p. 286].

A Relationship: Yes or No?

General

Object of This Card Divination

If you are uncertain whether or not to enter a relationship, with this card divination pattern you may determine what is the right decision for you.

Getting into the Right Mood

Sometimes we encounter people who leave us uncertain in regards to whether we should have a relationship with them or not. We do not feel quite ready yet. Or we are afraid of commitment. We fear to hurt someone or to experience another disappointment. We do not know whether he or she is the right one. Something prevents us from entering this relationship, yet we cannot say what it is. Question yourself: what is stopping me from really saying yes? Is it me, or is it because of the experience of earlier relationships? Or is it the other person? Does something disturb me? Am I missing something? Am I afraid to hurt or be hurt? What do I need to be able to enter this relationship? Is he or she the partner for life or not? How do I feel when imagining a relationship with this person? What might I feel if I stay single? What moves me? Which questions occupy me concerning this person? What do I want?

Base

Card Divination Pattern

General (Foundation)

    1. Central theme: The relationship
    2. My hidden theme with relationships
    3. What happens if I say yes?
    4. What happens if I say no?
    5. What prevents me from entering this relationship?
    6. What needs to be done or left alone?
    7. Does this encounter have a future?
    8. What is the chance of development at this point?

Companion

Base (Elemental power)

    9. Which natural force accompanies me if I say yes?
    10. Which natural force accompanies me if I say no?

Companion (Support)

    11. What accompanies me if I say yes?
    12. What accompanies me if I say no?
    13. What gives me strength now?

Master

Master (Apprenticeship)

    14. Under which star does our union stand?

Joker (Surprise)

    15. What helps me if I say yes?
    16. What helps me if I say no?
    17. What is the special gift during this time?

Joker

Tip/Advice

If you wish to deepen the subject, you may continue working with other patterns, such as, The Inner Woman [see p. 74], The Inner Man [see p. 76], The Inner Couple [see p. 78], The Inner Child [see p. 72], and Relationship to Oneself [see p. 70].

A Change of Partner: Yes or No?

General

Object of This Card Divination
With this card divination pattern, the possibility of a radical change in partnership can be examined more thoroughly.

Getting into the Right Mood

Base

Partnership is the smallest form of community. It ensures an intensive closeness to one another. However, if this closeness no longer corresponds with one's inner experience of the relationship, the partnership can then be the cause of great loneliness. One has expected something quite different from the partner and this expectation has not been fulfilled. The couple does not get along. Things are no longer as they were in the beginning. The individual no longer recognizes the other who is supposed to share in life. The other has drifted apart. These kinds of thoughts and inner experiences are often the reason for wondering if the relationship should be ended. It could also be that love has flowered with another person and we are uncertain which way to go. A relationship is exposed to eternal change like everything else that lives. It develops and has its good and bad times. There are phases during which it sickens or during which nothing progresses. Yet this does not have to be a reason to give up on it. For such phases can be temporary appearances that indicate that the relationship is altering, has difficulties in growing, or is making no progress. During such times, partners begin to examine their relationship to one another, to assess it, and to reevaluate it, and to sometimes give it up.

Companion

Concentrate on your momentary situation. What does the old partnership continue to give to you? What does the relationship take from you? Where would it have to change in your opinion? Does it still possess the opportunity to develop further? What are you missing? What attracts you to a new partner?

Card Divination Pattern

Master

General (Foundation)
1. Central theme/relationship
2. What makes me stay with my old partner?
3. What attracts me to a new partner?
4. What happens if I stay?
5. What happens if I leave?
6. What needs to be done?
7. What is helping me at this point?
8. What is my chance for development in this situation?
9. How will I benefit from this development?

Joker

Base (Elemental Power)
10. Which natural force is assisting me now?

Companion (Support)

11. Which force stands by my side if I stay?
12. Which force stands by my side if I leave?
13. Which force can I call in difficult situations?

Master (Apprenticeship)

14. Under which star is this moment standing?

Joker (Surprise)

15. What is helping me at this point?
16. What helps me in difficult situations?

Tip/Advice

In order to build up your knowledge, you may continue working with The Inner Couple [see p. 78], The Inner Man [see p. 76], The Inner Woman [see p. 74], Crisis [see p. 130], and Blind Spot [see p. 134] card divination patterns.

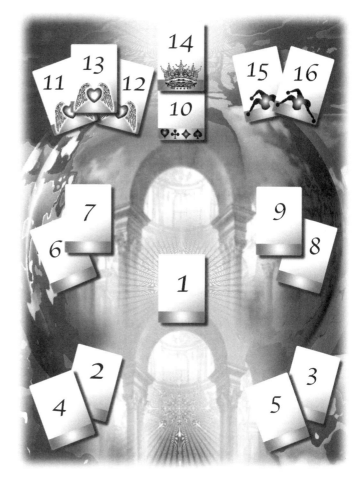

Heartache and Lovesickness

General

Object of This Card Divination

With this card divination pattern, you can examine your heartache or your lovesickness more closely.

Getting into the Right Mood

> "He loves me, he loves me not; she loves me, she loves me not."

Base

Sometimes, our desires and our dreams are not fulfilled by a partner or in a relationship; they may even be destroyed or broken. We feel attracted to somebody, but he or she does not want to reciprocate as this person might feel friendship rather than love. We are dumped because someone else is more "attractive." We spend a certain amount of time with a person, since we are meant to fulfill a certain task together, and afterward everyone goes his or her way once again. We go awhile together as, in this way, we mutually foster our development. Then, we separate once more because each of our developments take a different direction: we have a fateful encounter with a person with whom we still have to solve or to learn something. There are countless possibilities for encounters, disappointments, heartache, and lovesickness.

Companion

Here are some questions for attuning yourself: What am I grieving for? What was the force that served us well? What is the reason why our love could not be lived? What did I see in the other person that is lacking in my life? How did I benefit from the encounter? What did the encounter take away from me? What is the background of this encounter?

Card Divination Pattern

General (Foundation)

1. Central theme: Heartache
2. The hidden theme
3. The forbidden theme

Master

4. What did the other person give to me?
5. What did the other person take away from me?
6. What is the force in the encounter?
7. Which gift lies in this encounter?
8. What do I have to let go now?
9. What needs to be done or left alone?
10. Does the relationship have a future?
11. What is my current chance for development?

Joker

Base (Elemental power)

12. Which natural force needs to be observed in particular?

Companion (Support)

13. What is standing by my side at this point?
14. What force will be there for me in painful situations?

Master (Apprenticeship)

15. Under which cosmic influence does this encounter stand?

Joker (Surprise)

16. What is helping me now, what is healing me now?

17. What is helping me with my lovesickness at this point?

18. What is the special gift during this time?

Tip/Advice

Allow the cards to have an effect on you for some time. In situations in which we feel pain, we often do not want to accept the cards' message immediately. Therefore, give yourself some time until you have absorbed the message of the cards deep inside of you. The words of the Dalai Lama might provide you with some comfort: "Remember that not getting what you want is sometimes a wonderful stroke of luck."

General

The Specialness of the Relationship

Object of This Card Divination

This card divination pattern is there for checking up on a relationship. You may carry it out alone or as a couple.

Getting into the Right Mood

> *"Everyone gets the partner that he or she deserves."* (Hermann Meyer)

Base

Our relationships do not come into being just like that. We choose our partners according to conscious and unconscious criteria. One's inner reality is reflected in the relationship. Ask yourself (you must all ask yourselves): What is the quality of our relationship? What can we give to one another? What can we offer the world? What can we not give to ourselves? Where do we support one another? Where do we hinder one another? What can we learn together? Attune yourself to the subject, and then begin laying out the cards.

Card Divination Pattern

General (Foundation)

Companion

1. Our relationship
2. The hidden theme of our partnership
3. The forbidden theme of our partnership
4. Our common base
5. How do I view the relationship?
6. How does my partner view the relationship?
7. My contribution
8. My partner's contribution
9. What do I see in my partner?
10. What does my partner see in me?
11. What do we reflect from within ourselves?
12. My chance for development in our relationship
13. My partner's chance for development
14. Our common chance for development
15. What are our prospects for the future?

Base (Elemental power)

16. Which natural force needs to be particularly observed in our relationship?

Companion (Support)

17. Which cosmic force stands by my side?
18. Which cosmic force stands by my partner's side?
19. Which force helps us in difficult situations?

Master (Apprenticeship)

Joker

20. Under which star does our relationship stand?
21. Which cosmic force comes into this world through our union?

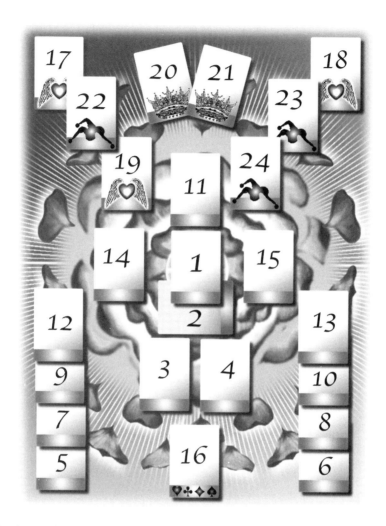

Joker (Surprise)

    22. What helps and heals me?

    23. What helps and heals my partner?

    24. What helps and heals our relationship?

Tip/Advice

The theme can be given more depth with these card divination patterns: The Inner Woman [see p. 74], The Inner Man [see p. 76], The Inner Couple [see p. 78], The Karmic Connection [see p. 50], and The Principle of Correspondence [see p. 258].

Couple Talk

General

Object of This Card Divination
This card divination pattern is meant for couples. It can be the base for a good exchange between the partners.

Getting into the Right Mood
Create a comfortable atmosphere. Light a candle, and simply take some time for one another to sit together and talk in-depth. Often, we are so occupied with everyday affairs that we do not take the time to really talk to one another. Use the opportunity and have a good conversation.

Base

Here are some questions for attuning yourselves: What has occupied me/you recently? How are you/am I/we doing? What is nice in our life? What is nice about you; what is nice about me? What are you/am I/are we lacking? What is good for us/you/me and what is not? What is currently on the agenda? Decide upon the cards with which you would like to work, and then begin laying them out.

Card Divination Pattern
General (Foundation)
1. Partner A: That is how I see you (B)
2. Partner B: That is how I see you (A)
3. Partner A: That is how I see myself
4. Partner B: That is how I see myself

Companion

5. Partner A: That is how I see our relationship
6. Partner B: That is how I see our relationship
7. Partner A: That to which I should pay attention
8. Partner B: That to which I should pay attention
9. The secret
10. Our happiness
11. What lies ahead of us

Base (Elemental power)
12. Partner A: This natural force needs to be particularly observed with me
13. Partner B: This natural force needs to be particularly observed with me

Companion (Support)
14. Partner A: This accompanies me
15. Partner B: This accompanies me
16. What accompanies our relationship

Master (Apprenticeship)
17. Our relationship stands under this star at the moment

Joker (Surprise)
18. What supports and strengthens us

19. Partner A: That is the gift to you (A)
20. Partner B: That is the gift to you (B)

Tip/Advice

In order to give the subject more depth, you may work with The Inner Couple card divination pattern [see p. 78].

Relationship Analysis

Object of This Card Divination

With this card divination pattern you can examine and understand a partnership/relationship more thoroughly.

Getting into the Right Mood

When two team up, a third thing always results from it. It is called partnership or marriage. Each relationship has its very own spirit, its very own being. At the beginning, this being lives upon what the two people brought with them and what led them together in the first place: affection, sympathy and love. These are the forces that attract, that build up the "spirit of the relationship." After some time, however, these forces that were brought into the relationship no longer have the same measure of effect. The being must have care and attention lavished on so that it can grow and thrive even further. The partnership "being" undergoes a development equaling a human being. It grows, becomes larger, overcomes obstacles, and experiences many phases of development to mature. Thus, it is important to seek again and again for true conversation and connection, and then to strengthen it, to protect it and to maintain it.

Base

Companion

Here are some questions for attuning yourself: Where do I stand, where does my partner stand? What is going on with our relationship? Which development are we going through? Which inauguration do we experience? What have we learned together? Is our "relationship being" viable and strong, or is it sick and so must be nurtured? What has developed between us? What has fallen by the wayside? What should be practiced once again? What is important to us? What is not so important to us? What expectations and fears are there? It is good to converse actively, to truly listen to the other person and to contribute to the meaningful development of this relationship and partnership "being."

Card Divination Pattern

Master

General (Foundation)

    1. Central theme of the relationship

    2. Me

    3. My partner

    4. What is the base of our partnership?

    5. My expectations

    6. My fears

    7. My partner's expectations

    8. My partner's fears

    9. The strengths of our union

   10. The weaknesses of our union

   11. What can be changed?

   12. What should be avoided?

   13. Which path of development does this partnership take?

Joker

Base (*Elemental power*)
14. The natural force that needs to be particularly observed in our partnership

Companion (*Support*)
15. The force that accompanies our partnership
16. The force that supports our partnership in difficult times
17. The force that helps us now in this phase of development

Master (*Apprenticeship*)
18. The star under which our union stands

Joker (*Surprise*)
19. What I need/what heals me
20. What my partner needs/what heals my partner
21. What supports our relationship/ heals it

Tip/Advice

If one wishes to analyze this topic in even greater detail, then The Inner Man [see p. 76] and The Inner Woman [see p. 74] card divination patterns provide a good possibility. You may also want to have a look at the card divination patterns in the Hermetic Principles chapter [see pp. 256–269] in regards to relationship.

Marriage
Starting a Family: Yes or No?

General

Object of This Card Divination
With this card divination pattern you can both examine and understand a partnership/relationship more thoroughly.

Getting into the Right Mood

Base

"But let there be spaces in your togetherness, and let the winds of heaven dance between you. Love one another, but make not a bond of love; Let it rather be a moving sea between the shores of your soul" (Khalil Gibran, The Prophet)

Marriage is a risk. A certain level of maturity is needed in marriage as well as an ability to adhere to promises. Two people come together in marriage in order to go through life as a unity, as husband and wife. With our traditional ceremony, the partners promise one another to stand by each other's side in good and in bad times. Marriage is an educational path, one of the opening paths of today's time. An individual learns to grow beyond the self, to make sacrifices, to be together there for others, to develop compassion and care, to love unconditionally. Before people say yes to marriage, they should thoroughly examine if they

Companion

are really ready for this step; a person should further examine if a completeness is felt and if others can be cared for with power and love.

You can lay this spread alone or together with your partner. Ask yourself/all of you ask yourselves: Do I feel ready to go through life together with someone? What is my motivation for this decision? Do I feel ready to possibly take on responsibility for children? What is important to me? What do I wish to contribute to marriage? What do I expect from my partner? What are my imaginations, anxieties, wishes and dreams?

Attune yourself/ yourselves to the theme and then begin laying out the cards.

Master

Card Divination Pattern
General (Foundation)
1. Central theme: Marriage/planning a family
2. The hidden theme/background
3. The motivation for this step
4. The Base, the root, the Base for marriage/for planning a family
5. On the one hand
6. On the other hand
7. What happens if one enters into marriage at this point?
8. What happens if one does not enter into marriage at this point?
9. Anxieties
10. Wishes
11. What needs to be done or left alone now?
12. Where is our chance for development at this moment?

Joker

13. What are our prospects for the future?

Base *(Elemental power)*

14. Which natural force needs to be particularly observed?

Companion *(Support)*

15. What stands by our side if we enter into marriage?

16. What stands by our side if we do not enter into marriage at this point?

17. What is helping us with our decision right now?

Master *(Apprenticeship)*

18. What does the cosmos say to it?

Joker *(Surprise)*

19. What is helping and supporting us right now?

20. What does the oracle say about it?

Tip/Advice

Should the need arise, you may continue working with The Inner Couple [see p. 78] or The Small Fork [see p. 36] card divination pattern.

Families: The Primal Family

General

Object of This Card Divination

Here, you can spiritually attempt to come to terms with the family and its structure from which you originated and then start to recognize possible obstacles and entanglements.

Getting into the Right Mood

"If the husband is indeed a husband and the wife is wife, if the father is truly a father and the son a son, if the older brother holds his seat as the older brother and the younger sister hers of a younger sister, then the family is in order. When the family is in order, thus, all the social relationships of mankind will be in order." (*From the I Ching: "The Family"*)

Base

Take some time for yourself. Think about your family. How is your relationship with your parents, with your mother, with your father? What have they given you on your way through life? Which relatives are close to you? With which do you have a good relationship, and which ones do you dislike? What is the theme in the female and what in the male line of your family? What is the force, the symbol of your female or male line respectively? What have you adopted in regards to patterns, standards, and values? Which peculiarities exist in your family? How do you regard the relationship of these to yourself? How is your relationship to life? What troubles you? What do you like? As soon as you have attuned yourself to the subject, you may begin laying out the cards.

Companion

Card Divination Pattern

General (*Foundation*)

1. The theme in the family
2. My father/my relationship to my father
3. My mother/my relationship to my mother
4. Where applicable: My siblings/my relationship with my siblings (one card each per sister or brother, starting from the oldest to the youngest)
5. Theme of the father's family
6. Theme of the mother's family

Master

7. How I see myself
8. How I am regarded/my position in the family
9. The family secret
10. The family happiness
11. What do I need to solve?

Base (*Elemental power*)

12. Which natural force needs to be particularly observed in our family?

Joker

Companion (*Support*)

13. The force which accompanies our family
14. The force which is accompanying me right now

Master (*Apprenticeship*)

    15. The higher significance of the family subject

Joker (*Surprise*)

    16. What is helping me right now and what is healing me?

    17. What needs to be done?

Tip/Advice

Each family has its very own history and tradition. If you look into the mirror of your family, you will recognize a part of yourself.

Families: The Contemporary Family

General

Object of This Card Divination

With this card divination pattern, you can spiritually come to terms with your current family situation. By doing so, you might possibly recognize themes that should be worked on.

Getting into the Right Mood

Base

Take some time for yourself. Think about your current family. If you are two or more in the family, you may discuss the family situation. Each one of you should give some thought to the following questions: what is my case history? When did I meet my partner? How much time have we spent together? How do I feel about my current family? Do I feel comfortable or constricted? Am I doing fine? How do I get along with my/our child/children? What makes me happy? What burdens me? Where do we stick together; where do our ways separate? Which theme is fulfilled, which one is not? Am I able to recognize some of the patterns of my earlier family in my current family? How do I behave toward my partner, the children, and myself? If each of you has attuned to the theme and has decided which decks should be used, then begin laying out the cards.

Card Divination Pattern

Companion

General (Foundation)
1. The theme/our family's themes
2. That's how I see myself in the family
3. That's how I see myself individually
4. That's how I see my partner
5. We as a couple
6. We as parents
7. Our child/our children (for each child a card, starting from the oldest to the youngest)

Master

8. My relationship to the children
9. My partner's relationship to the children
10. What I have brought along from my family (from my parents)
11. What my partner brought along from his or her family (from his/her parents)
12. What makes me/us happy?
13. What burdens me/us?
14. What needs to be solved? (What do I/we need to solve? On what should I/we work? What needs to be reappraised?)

Joker

Base (Elemental power)
15. The natural force that needs to be particularly observed in our family

Companion (Support)

16. What accompanies and protects our family life?
17. What accompanies and protects our relationship as a couple?
18. What accompanies and protects our children? (You may draw a Companion for each child.)
19. What accompanies and protects me? (Here, everyone who participates can draw a card.)

Joker (Surprise)

20. What supports and heals our family life?
21. What assists us further?

Master (Apprenticeship)

22. Under which star does the happiness of our family stand?

Tip/Advice

This card divination pattern can be nicely laid out with two or, if the children are older, with the entire family. Each "player" may draw a card to the individual points and speak what comes to his or her mind. It is also possible to alternate with the drawing of the cards. If something is unclear, the Blind Spot [see p. 134] or Clarifying Ambiguous Cards [see p. 44] card divination patterns can assist further.

Relationship to Oneself

General

Object of This Card Divination

With this card divination pattern, you can observe how you stand in relation to yourself.

Getting into the Right Mood

"Love thy neighbor, as thyself" (Jesus Christ)

Self-acceptance and self-love are preconditions for a healthy relationship. For how are you supposed to give something to someone else, if you cannot even give it to yourself?

Base

Take some time and think about yourself. How do you feel about your own person? How has your life been up to this point? What gives you strength? What takes your strength? How well have you been able to know yourself? Do you listen to yourself, to your inner feeling? What are your abilities? What are your weaknesses? How do you see yourself? What have you made of your life up to this point? What do you still wish to make of it? Where are you in peace with yourself and where not? When you have attuned yourself to this subject, begin laying out the cards. Work with those card decks that correspond best with your own being.

Card Divination Pattern

Companion

General (Foundation)

1. My own being
   1a. Subconscious
   1b. Consciousness
   1c. Uber-conscious/my higher self
2. My strengths
3. My weaknesses
4. How I see myself
5. How others see me

Master

6. What makes me happy?
7. What shocks me?
8. What I treat with contempt
9. What I have to let go
10. What can strengthen me
11. What I have brought along
12. What I carry within me due to my education
13. What I am
14. What I can

Joker

15. What I want
16. Where my life leads me to

Base (Elemental power)

17. The natural force that works particularly strongly through me

Companion (*Support*)

    18. What is strengthening and supporting me now

Joker (*Surprise*)

    19. What heals me/the core of my being

Master (*Apprenticeship*)

    20. The star under which my journey through life stands right now

Tip/Advice

If the cards seem unclear to you, you may work with the Clarifying Ambiguous Cards [see p. 44] card divination pattern.

The Inner Child

General

Object of This Card Divination

Through this work with The Inner Child card divination pattern, you will get in touch with the long-ago days of your childhood, the wonderful experiences and the not-so-great ones of that time. This card divination pattern opens the gate to your inner child, and you may begin to recognize the things that are hidden within its kingdom.

Getting into the Right Mood

Base

"There was a time, where flowers, meadows, creeks and trees seemed to be bathed in a heavenly light. Everything astonished you, caused you to halt and to pause. This is a journey to that which you once brought with you into this world. [...] Your ability to take things in, your spontaneity, your inventiveness, and your deeply felt joy; your ability to dream, to fly with the birds; the liberty of the strength to live in the here and now, and the liberty to recognize the moment. Sometimes, it is not a simple path to open this door. Too much has happened in those days. Yet the child in you lives and waits for you to open the door of your heart once again." (Bluestar in: The Presence of Masters)

Companion

Many of us have only few memories left from childhood. Yet, there lies a force hidden within that can be reborn. If you meditate upon your own inner child, the child inside of you, you can recognize what has happened with this force and how you can activate it once again.

Here are some questions for attuning yourself: Which memories do I have of my childhood? What were the decisive experiences? Where did my heart widen? Where did my heart close up? Which people, circumstances, and subjects shaped my childhood? What do I feel when I look at a photo of my childhood? What do I still have with me from my childhood days? Attune yourself with these questions, choose your cards, and then begin laying them out.

Master

Card Divination Pattern

General (Foundation)

1. Where do I come from?
2. Where do I go?
3. What is the hidden/secret theme of my childhood?
4. What is the central theme of my childhood?
5. What have I brought along?
6. What are my roots/what is my Base?

Joker

7+ 8. What did I experience in my childhood (on the one hand/on the other hand)?
9. How do I see my inner child?
10. What needs to be worked on/done right now?
11. What needs to be put to rest?
12. What continues to hinder me?

13. What have I learned from it?
14. What can heal, resolve, or develop now?

Base (Elemental power)
15. Which natural force needs to be particularly observed regarding my inner child?

Companion (Support)
16. Which force has accompanied me since my childhood?
17. Which force is helping and healing my inner child now?

Master (Apprenticeship)
18. Under which star do my childhood days stand?
19. Which force leads me now?

Joker (Surprise)
20. What helps me in the contact with my inner child?

Tip/Advice

In order to grant this theme more depth, you may work with the Hermetic Principles patterns [see pp. 256–269]. Also, the Birth to Age 7 [see p. 150] and Destiny of Life [see p. 186] card divination patterns can help you further in this respect.

General

The Inner Woman

Object of This Card Divination

With this card divination pattern, you may examine the picture of your inner woman, the female dimension inside of you, more closely.

Getting into the Right Mood

We all consist of female and male dimensions. No matter whether we are man or woman, here we can work with the female part within us. Our image of the female part is shaped by our inner attitude, by our experiences, and by our way of life, our encounter with this female side. Our dedication, our ability to impress, our intuition, our earth and our water, our emotional activities, our passive side, silence, listening, patience, our night, all our hidden things are part of our female side. Through the female part in us, we can receive, empathize, understand, let things happen, accept, let go, and exhale.

Base

Here are some questions for attuning oneself: What is the picture of your female aspect? How does the female part manifest itself? How do you use the female force inside of you? Which image do you have of this force? How do you choose to express it with your signature style? What is the state of your care, your compassion? What are your female strengths, your female weaknesses? Attune yourself with these questions to the subject, choose your cards, and then begin laying them out.

Companion

Card Divination Pattern

General (Foundation)

    1. My inner woman/the female side

    2. What picture do I have of my inner woman/the female side?

    3. What is the true nature of my inner woman/the inner side?

  4. + 5. What needs to be observed on the one hand/on the other hand?

    6. What is my feeling, my intuition, my element of water?

    7. What is my care, my gift, my element of water?

    8. On what do I have to work?

    9. Where does my inner woman/the female side in me strengthen/weaken me?

   10. Which picture, which conviction of my inner woman/the female side should I give up?

   11. How can I use my inner woman/the female side within me in my life?

Base (Elemental power)

   12. Which natural force needs to be observed in regards to my female side?

Companion (Support)

   13. Which force accompanies my inner woman/the female side?

Master (Apprenticeship)

   14. Under which star does my inner woman/the female side stand?

Master

Joker

Joker (*Surprise*)

    15. Which force strengthens/heals my inner woman/the female side?

Tip/Advice

In order to give this theme more depth, you may continue working with The Element of Earth [see p. 120], The Element of Water [see p. 118], The Principle of Gender [see p. 268], and The Inner Couple [see p. 78] card divination patterns.

The Inner Man

General

Object of This Card Divination

With this card divination pattern, you may examine the picture of your inner man, the male part inside of you, more closely.

Getting into the Right Mood

We all consist of male and female dimensions. No matter whether we are man or woman, here we can work with the male part within us. Our image of the male part is shaped by our

Base

inner attitude, by our experiences, and by our way of life, our encounter with this male side. Our activity, our ability to express ourselves, our energy, our fire and our air, our mental activities, our self-assessment, our day side. Through the male part in us, we are able to express ourselves, to show ourselves, to appear, to be active, to hold on, and to inhale.

Here are some questions for attuning oneself: How do you picture your male dimension? What is the picture of the male force? How do you use your male strength inside of you? How do you express yourself in the world? How do you function within the group? What are your male strengths, your male weaknesses?

Companion

Card Divination Pattern

General (Foundation)

1. My inner man/the male side
2. Which picture do I have of my inner man/the male side?
3. How is he really?

4. + 5. What needs to be observed on the one hand/on the other hand?

6. What is my strength, my force, my element of fire?
7. What is my mind, my thinking, my element of air?
8. On what do I have to work?

Master

9. Where does my inner man/the male side strengthen/weaken me?
10. Which conviction of my inner man/the male side should I give up?
11. How can I use my inner man/the male side in my life?

Base (Elemental power)

12. Which natural force needs to be observed in regards to my inner man/male side?

Companion (Support)

13. Which force accompanies my inner man/the male side?

Master (Apprenticeship)

14. Under which star does my inner man/the male side stand?

Joker (Surprise)

15. Which force strengthens/heals my inner man/the male side?

Joker

Tip/Advice

In order to give more depth to this subject, you may continue working with The Element of Fire [see p. 122], The Element of Air [see p. 116], The Principle of Gender [see p. 168], and The Inner Couple [see p. 78] card divination patterns.

The Inner Couple

General

Object of This Card Divination

With this card divination pattern, you may examine how your male and female portions stand in relation to one another, for, as it is on the outside, thus it is on the inside; and so as exists your inner couple, thus exists your outer couple.

Getting into the Right Mood

The idea of your inner couple is reflected in the outside. If you wish to understand why your partnerships tend to run the way the way they do, why you time and again attract the same type of man/woman, try working with your inner couple.

Base

Ask yourself: How does your female side look; how does your male side look? How is their relationship to one another? How are your inner imaginations of man and woman, of male and female? How do your inner woman and your inner man relate to one another? Do both have a lot in common? Does their contact only concentrate on certain areas? Do they even get along at all? Occupy yourself with your idea of your inner couple. In this context, you will certainly find many keys and answers for what you experience in your life and in your relationships.

Card Divination Pattern

Companion

General (Foundation)
    1. Central subject/the inner couple/the inner union
    2. My male side
    3. My female side
    4. Needs of the male side
    5. Needs of the female side
    6. Central theme of the male side
    7. Central theme of the female side

Master

    8. What unites both parts?
    9. What separates both parts?
    10. What needs to be changed?
    11. What helps and heals?
Base (Elemental power)
    12. Which natural force fosters or hinders the inner partnership?
Companion (Support)
    13. What accompanies my female side?
    14. What accompanies my male side?

Joker

    15. What accompanies my inner couple?
Master (Apprenticeship)
    16. What unites my inner couple?
Joker (Surprise)
    17. What heals my female side?

18. What heals my male side?

19. What heals and supports the inner couple?

Tip/Advice

In order to gain more depth with this theme, you may work with The Inner Man [see p. 76], The Inner Woman [see p. 74], The Principle of Gender [see p. 268], and The Principle of Correspondence [see p. 258] card divination patterns.

General

Partnership Complications
Profession, Friendship, Partnership

Object of This Card Divination
This card divination pattern serves to examine those partnership entanglements that can happen in professional life.

Getting into the Right Mood

Base

When, for example, a couple or friends work together, if they establish a common enterprise, complications can easily arise, as several relationship levels are overlapping. Here, the individual should examine the crucial issues: What belongs to our personal relationship? What belongs to our work relationship? In other words: What is business, and what is friendship? Separating these things can once again bring clarity into the matter.

Attune yourself alone or with the appropriate partner. The following questions will help you with this: Where are you professionally bound together? Where are you bound in private? How are earnings and expenses handled, both in your private and in your business life? What is the level of work matters? What is the relationship level? In what areas do these levels mix? What would you like from one another? What is your idea? What ideas does the other person have?

Companion

Card Divination Pattern
General (Foundation)
1. Central theme/general situation
2. Me
3. My partner
4. Our common base
5. Our secret connection
6. Our private relationship
7. Our professional relationship
8. Where does our relationships entangle? Where do complications arise?
9. This habit helps or hinders me
10. This habit helps or hinders my partner
11. This is beneficial or disturbing for us
12. On this we need to work
13. This is what the future will bring for us

Base (Elemental power)
14. This natural force needs to be observed on a private level
15. This natural force needs to be observed on a professional level

Joker

Companion (Support)
16. This accompanies us in private
17. This accompanies us in our professional life
18. This helps us in difficult and complicated situations

Master *(Apprenticeship)*

    19. Our union currently stands under this cosmic force

    20. We can call upon this cosmic force in complicated situations

Joker *(Surprise)*

    21. This helps us in private

    22. This helps us in our professional life

    23. This helps us in difficult and complicated situations

Tip/Advice

Should the need arise, you may continue working with The Karmic Connection [see p. 50], Blind Spot [see p. 134], The Eisenhower Method [see p. 42] or with other patterns.

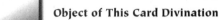

Career Oracle

Vocation

Object of This Card Divination
With this card divination pattern, you can find out what your calling is and what you should pursue as your profession.

Getting into the Right Mood
A profession is more than just a job that gets you some money. A profession is a vocation; it is your inner calling and your life's task. If you follow your calling, this inner vocation, then you will find happiness and richness in every aspect. We all have endowments, those things we know that we like to do from the heart, and those things that we do not like at all. We all have inclinations toward one direction or the other. One likes to travel, while the other prefers to remain firmly on the same spot. One finds joy in math, the other learns languages easily, and still the next one is musical. As adults, we spend a great deal of our time in our profession, and so it is important that we hear this inner calling and follow through on what fulfills us and makes us happy and content.

Base

Here are some questions for attuning yourself: What are your abilities? What do you like to do? What comes easy to you? Which dogmas or convictions do you carry inside of you that might prevent you from following your calling? For example, do you think that work should not be fun; or that fulfillment is not to be found in work because your parents were not allowed to experience this either; or is work only there to make money, as life truly begins with leisure? Occupy yourself with this topic. Make a list of everything you like to do and of what you do not like to do.

Companion

Card Divination Pattern
General (Foundation)
   1. Base/Basis
   2. Central theme/my vocation
   3. On the one hand
   4. On the other hand
   5. My desires
   6. My endowments
   7. My anxieties
   8. My power of fate
   9. What needs to be done/left alone?
   10. What happens if I follow my most inner desire/my vocation?
   11. Professional future

Base (Elemental power)
   12. Which natural force needs to be particularly observed?

Companion (Support)
   13. Which force supports me if I follow my vocation?

Master

Joker

14. Which force supports me in difficult situations?

Master (Apprenticeship)

15. Under which star does my professional desire stand?

Joker (Surprise)

16. Which force is helping me?

17. What does the oracle say about this?

Tip/Advice

To explore this in more depth, you may continue working with The Great Fork [see p. 38] card divination pattern.

Game of Fate

The Solution to the Problem

Object of This Card Divination

This card divination pattern serves to examine more closely the reasons why fate has led you to your current situation.

Getting into the Right Mood

Sometimes fate leads us to reflect upon our situation in life. We get into serious difficulties. For instance, we are in danger of losing our job, business is not going well, we are up to our ears in debt, or we get sick. However, nothing in our life happens coincidentally or randomly even if it might look like it. All that we encounter belongs to our fate, for it would not be on our path otherwise. These circumstances belong to our chances of learning and growth.

Problems are there to be solved. If you are in a difficult situation, ask yourself the following questions: What got me into this situation? What has recently dictated my thinking and my feeling? What are the circumstances at this moment? In what matters was my determination lacking? What needs to be done now; and which solutions and possibilities present themselves? What am I supposed to learn from this situation; what message does this situation have in store for me; what is the task of this current situation? What needs to be solved within me now? Am I following my vocation or not; did I perhaps miss an inner calling? You may also take a sheet of paper and write down your deepest fears and then transform each fear into its positive counterpart. Consciously decide for responsibility and happiness in your life.

Card Divination Pattern

General (Foundation)

1. Central theme/my problem
2. The hidden side of the problem
3. The message of the current situation
4. power of fate/ influence of fate
5. What I should observe
6. My task at that moment
7. The alternative
8. The chance for growth
9. The development for the moment

Base (Elemental power)

10. The natural force that needs to be particularly observed

Companion (Support)

11. The force that stands by my side
12. The force that helps me to solve the problem/to understand the message

Master (*Apprenticeship*)

    13. The cosmic influence in the current situation

Joker (*Surprise*)

    14. This helps me with the solution of the problem

    15. That is what the oracle says about it

    16. The gift of the situation

Tip/Advice

To explore this in more depth, you may use the card divination patterns in The Principle of Correspondence [see p. 258] and The Principle of Spirituality [see p. 256]. Additionally, you may use Crisis [see p. 130], Blind Spot [see p. 134], and the other methods described in the Self-knowledge and Healing chapter [see pp. 128–147].

Career Decision

Should I Pursue New Paths?

Object of This Card Divination

This card divination pattern helps you when you are going through a change in your professional life or when new opportunities are opening up in a professional respect.

Getting into the Right Mood

There are often periods in a one's professional life when dissatisfaction with a situation begins to grow. If this happens, it is time to check how things are supposed to continue. Dissatisfaction is a safe sign of the need for growth and development. Use such times to reconsider your professional situation and even possibly consider a new path. What speaks for the old path? What speaks for a new path? Am I still able to develop myself in my profession/in my company/in my environment? Can I still grow here? What possibilities do I have? You may take a few notes and then begin laying out the cards.

Card Divination Pattern

General (Foundation)

1. My current professional situation
2. What lies hidden
3. Because of this, I am satisfied/dissatisfied with the current situation
4. Because of this, my boss/my company/my work environment/my surrounding is dissatisfied with me
5. My inner desire
6. This happens if I follow new paths
7. This happens if I change nothing at all
8. This needs to be done now
9. This is my chance for development
10. This is awaiting me in the near future

Base (Elemental power)

11. This element needs to be particularly observed in this situation

Companion (Support)

12. This accompanies me if I pursue new directions
13. This accompanies me if I stay
14. This helps me in difficult situations

Master (Apprenticeship)

15. This is the cosmic influence during this time

Joker (Surprise)

16. This supports me if I pursue new directions
17. This supports me if I stay
18. This is what the oracle says about it

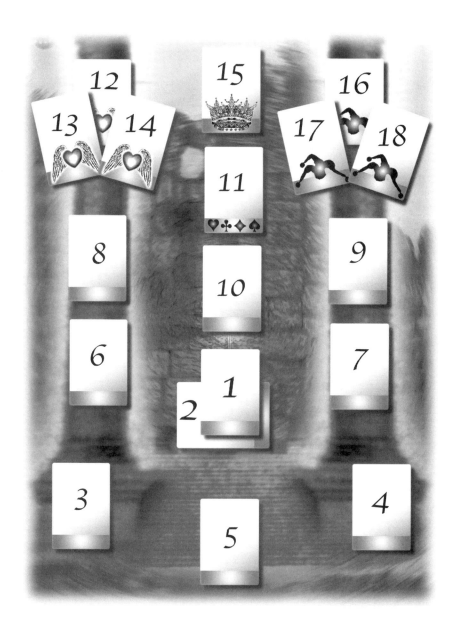

Tip/Advice

To explore this in more depth, you may continue to work with other oracle techniques. The Higher Position card divination pattern [see p. 88] can help here as well.

General

The Higher Position
Should I Take the Opportunity Offered or Not?

Object of This Card Divination
This card divination pattern is suitable in any situation in which you strive for a higher position, a promotion in your professional life.

Getting into the Right Mood
Here are some questions for attuning yourself: Should I go for the higher position? Should I have myself nominated for the election? Should I accept the teaching position? Should I give presentations? Should I apply for a promotion? Should I hold seminars? Should I become self-employed? Should I accept the position? Should I quit my job? Should I open my own business? Should I go for further education? Should I strive for this field of study? Should I go back to work? If one of the questions appeals to you, then this is the right card divination pattern in order to grapple with this issue in greater detail.

Base

Card Divination Pattern
General (Foundation)

Companion

1. Central theme
2. My base, my foundation
3. My desires
4. My objections
5. What are my abilities/my preconditions?
6. What can I give?
7. What do I still have to learn?
8. What do I have to sacrifice?
9. What price will I pay for it?
10. What do I wish to achieve?
11. Do I have the ability to realize what I am imagining?
12. Temporary result/chance for development

Base (Elemental power)
13. Which natural force is helping me now?

Companion (Support)
14. What stands by my side in my current situation?
15. What stands by my side if I choose the new path?
16. What stands by my side in difficult situations?

Master (Apprenticeship)

Master

17. Under which cosmic influence do the present circumstances stand?

Joker (Surprise)

Joker

18. What does the oracle say about it?
19. What happens if I stay?
20. What happens if I choose a higher path?

Tip/Advice

If needed, you can examine this theme even more closely with The Small Fork card divination pattern [see p. 36].

Perfect Timing
A Plan of Success

General

Object of This Card Divination

There is a time for everything: a time for waiting, a time for acting, a favorable time and a less favorable time. With this card divination pattern, you can adopt a more critical look at your projects and see which forces are at work. You can find out what helps you, what you have to watch out for, and what prerequisites need to be present in order for your plan to succeed.

Base

Getting into the Right Mood

Take some time for yourself and concentrate on what you want to do. What exactly is your plan? You may take notes and get step by step clarity as to how you are going to put this plan into action. What is the driving force for this plan? What is its background; how did this plan arise? What do you wish to achieve with it; what is your goal? What do you need to achieve this goal; what needs to be done? What are the basic prerequisites for its success? Attune yourself to the subject and then begin laying out your cards of choice.

Companion

Card Divination Pattern

General (Foundation)

    1. The fundamental characteristic—a significant hint

    2. The driving force not yet known

    3. Confirmation or objections

    4. In this way it will succeed

    5. In this way it will not succeed

    6. This is important to observe

    7. This needs to be done or left alone

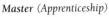
Master

    8. This is the prediction at this point

Base (Elemental power)

    9. This natural force needs to be observed with this project

Companion (Support)

    10. Under the influence of this force the project stands

    11. This force can help the project

Joker (Surprise)

    12. This is the fundamental characteristic seen from a higher perspective, the cosmic order that stands behind it.

Joker

    13. This is what the oracle says about the project

Master (Apprenticeship)

    14. Under this star the project stands

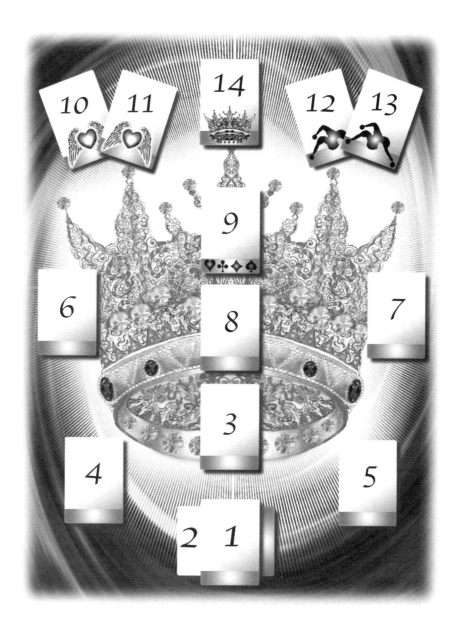

Tip/Advice

If you carry a vision or a plan inside of you, then the strength to put this plan into action also is carried within you.

Major Investments

General

Object of This Card Divination
With this card divination pattern you can examine whether the desired investments and acquisitions are the right ones or if it is even the right time for them.

Getting into the Right Mood
Major investments require a thorough examination, as they can cause costs over a longer period of time and may not yield what one has hoped for.

Base

With these questions, you can attune yourself to the subject: How and why did the thought arise to make this particular acquisition or investment? What do my feelings tell me? What is the purpose of this acquisition/investment? Which criteria must be fulfilled in order to make this investment? What do you have to watch out for? By doing so, what are the total costs especially those beyond mere purchase, such as notary fees, taxes, maintenance, etc.? Is this the right time? What other factors play a role? Find five positive arguments for the acquisition/investment as well as five negative arguments. Which other possibilities, alternatives, and sources exist which I have not thought of yet?

Take some time for yourself, and then find a slip of paper and a pen, and write everything down. If the acquisition/investment involves several people, then each person can answer the above-mentioned questions respectively and then confer with the other person(s) later on. As soon as the preparation is completed, you can begin laying out the cards after choosing them.

Companion

Card Divination Pattern
Base (Elemental power)
    1. Which natural force/elemental power supports me?
General (Foundation)
    2. Base/starting position
    3. How do I stand in relation to this huge acquisition/investment?
    4. Do I have the financial means?
    5. What needs to be done?
    6. What needs to be observed?
    7. Does the acquisition/investment fulfill my expectations?
Companion (Support)
    8. Which force supports the project?
Master (Apprenticeship)
    9. Under which star does the project stand?
Joker (Surprise)
    10. What helps me to make the decision right now?
    11. What does the oracle say about it?
    12. The unexpected

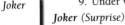

Master

Joker

Tip/Advice

If you wish to give this matter more depth, then the Blind Spot card divination pattern [see p. 134] can assist you further.

Seven Energy Wheels: The Chakras
General Survey

Object of This Card Divination

With this card divination pattern you can gain insight into the seven energy wheels, the so-called chakras, those seven main energy centers in your body that offer energy to the area to which they are ascribed. You will learn which chakras possess the greatest power and with which chakras you should work most intensively. In this way, you can recognize disturbances and strengths in your energy field and subsequently balance them out.

Base

Getting into the Right Mood

Here, you can work with anywhere from one to four card decks. Choose the decks, and then decide which deck serves as your foundation. Before you begin laying out the cards, concentrate on your energy system. How do you feel? Where do you feel something lacking? Where do you feel the most energy? Close your eyes, and become aware of the inner you. Ask yourself: How am I doing right now? First, read the short text of the respective chakra to yourself, then concentrate upon the chakra and afterward draw the card.

Companion

Card Divination Pattern

General (Foundation)

1. **Root Chakra (Muladhara Chakra)**
   Location: coccyx, pelvic floor between perineum and anus; color: red; themes: surviving, drive, material security, stability, base, grounding.
   Concentrate for about five minutes on the Root Chakra.
   Question for the card: Which force works in my Root Chakra?

2. **Sacral Chakra (Svadhisthana Chakra)**
   Location: area of the sacrum, above the sex organs; color: orange; themes: sexuality, reproduction, creativity, ability to build a good relationship with oneself and the environment.
   Concentrate for about five minutes on the Sacral Chakra.
   Question for the card: Which force works in my Sacral Chakra?

Master

3. **Navel Chakra (Manipura Chakra)**
   Location: above the navel, stomach area; color: golden yellow; themes: willpower, power, self-control, distribution of life energy through the body.
   Concentrate for about five minutes on your Navel Chakra.
   Question for the card: Which force works in my Navel Chakra?

4. **Heart Chakra (Anahata Chakra)**
   Location: heart level, center of the chest; colors: green, pink; themes: love, compassion, ability to love, security, warmth
   Concentrate for about five minutes on your Heart Chakra.
   Question for the card: Which force works in my Heart Chakra?

Joker

5. **Neck Chakra (Vishuddha Chakra)**
   Location: laryngopharynx, cervical vertebral column; color: blue; themes: union, communication, mental power, truth, ability to articulate oneself, and inspiration
   Concentrate for about five minutes on your Neck Chakra.
   Question for the card: Which force works in my Neck Chakra?

6. **Brow Chakra (Anja Chakra)**
   Location: between the eyebrows, above the bridge of the nose, in the middle of the forehead; colors: indigo blue, violet; themes: intuition, wisdom, immediate perception, inner sight
   Concentrate for about five minutes on your Brow Chakra.
   Question for the card: Which force works in my Brow Chakra?

7. **Crown Chakra (Sahasrara Chakra)**
   Location: top of the skull, vertex; colors: white, gold, rainbow colors; themes: cosmos, spirituality, mental worlds, illumination
   Concentrate for about five minutes on your Crown Chakra.
   Question for the card: Which force works in my Crown Chakra?
   Here, you can also draw a card from a master deck, for here the cosmos works.

Companion (Support)
8. + 9. Which forces of the cosmos accompany and support my energy system

Joker (Surprise) and/or Master (Apprenticeship): the quintessence
   10. Under which overall energy does my chakra system stand? What helps me to strengthen my energy system?

Tip/Advice
With this card divination pattern it is a good idea if you take some short notes so that you can think about it later. If the cards are negative, you can illuminate them with the card divination pattern Clarifying Ambiguous Cards [see p. 44] or you still draw two other cards with the questions: what is to be done? To what do I need to pay attention? For the respective chakra's healing cards, you may use other cards as well, such as, for example, Bach flower cards, herbal cards, Deva cards, and color cards. If you wish to learn more about the energy of a certain chakra, you may work with the individual chakra spreads on the following pages.

General

Root Chakra (Muladhara Chakra)

Base, Security, Stability

Object of This Card Divination

With this card divination pattern you learn more about the Root Chakra. The name Muladhara comes from the Sanskrit meaning "root" or "support." Your Root Chakra is the first main chakra and the basic center of your energy system. Your Root Chakra points to fundamental topics such as security, essential trust, stability, survival, and "rootedness." It nurtures the body, the spirit, and the soul with life energy and even secures survival.

Base

Getting into the Right Mood

Location: coccyx, pelvic floor between perineum and anus; colors: red; element: earth; symbol: square; planet: Mercury

Physical sphere of influence: skeleton, bones, legs, feet, coccyx, large intestine, end of your intestine

Healthy flow of energy: will to live, vitality, perseverance, rhythm, grounding and love of nature, staying power, ability to assert oneself, steadfastness, vigor, creative power, care

Physical disturbances of energy: backache, bone diseases, prostate suffering, varicose, constipation, hemorrhoids, gastrointestinal illnesses, blood-pressure fluctuation, anemia

Emotional disturbances of energy: egoism, lack of trust, depression, asthenia, lack of motivation, sluggishness, anxieties (particularly existential fears), domination by one's animal instincts, moodiness, imbalance

Companion

Here are some questions for attuning yourself: How does it look in regards to your stability, your staying power? How strong is your base? How is your contact with the earth? Concentrate for five to ten minutes on your Root Chakra. Which themes can you find here with you? Perhaps you could take some notes. When you have chosen your card decks, you may begin laying out the cards.

Master

Card Divination Pattern

General (Foundation)
1. My Root Chakra
2. Flow of energy
3. Blockage of energy
4. What helps me to ground myself?
5. What should I change or foster?

Companion (Support)
6. What accompanies me in my roots?
7. What helps me with blockages?

Joker

Joker (Surprise)
8. What helps me and heals me? What needs to be done in the near future?

Tip/Advice

If you wish to go on, then try working with The Element of Earth card divination pattern [see p. 120].

General

Sacral Chakra (Svadhisthana Chakra)

Sexuality, Creativity, Relations

Object of This Card Divination

With this card divination pattern you can learn more about your Sacral Chakra. The name Svadhisthana comes from the Sanskrit meaning "sweetness," suggesting the sensual and physical pleasures associated with this chakra. Your Sacral Chakra is the second main chakra within your energy system. Themes such as sexuality, procreation, the relationship with oneself and the environment, creativity, emotion and sentiment, love of life and sensuality all belong to this chakra.

Base

Getting into the Right Mood

Location: above the sexual organs, sacrum area; color: orange; element: water; symbol: crescent; planet: Venus

Physical sphere of influence: gonads, pelvic area, kidneys, bladder, circulation, body fluids, sexual and lower torso organs

Healthy influence: body consciousness, vitality, creativity, healing energy, passion, joy of life, female energy, creative power, expression, ability to have a relationship

Physical disturbances of energy: impotence, frigidity, kidneys and bladder problems, urinary tract infections, disease of blood and lymphs, menstruation problems

Companion

Emotional disturbances of energy: jealousy, domination by one's animal instincts, aggression, compulsion, feelings of guilt, fear of loss, dependence on one's sexual drive/addictive behavior, weakness, sexual disinterest, moodiness

Here are some questions for attuning yourself: What does your ability to have a relationship look like, and, similarly, how is your strength to connect with yourself and with your environment? Think further on your sensuality, your creativity, and your creative power. Concentrate for five to ten minutes on your Sacral Chakra. Which themes can you find here with you? You may wish to take some notes. After you have chosen your card decks, begin laying out your cards.

Master

Card Divination Pattern

General (Foundation)

1. My Sacral Chakra
2. Flow of energy
3. Blockage of energy
4. My relationship with myself
5. My trust in the world/my creative expression
6. What I am supposed to change or foster

Companion (Support)

7. This card strengthens my creative expressiveness/my creativity

Joker

Joker (Surprise)

8. This force heals and strengthens my joy of life

Tip/Advice

In regards to the blockages to your Sacral Chakra, you may draw yet another companion with the question: Which force helps me to overcome these obstacles?

If you wish to gain deeper insight, work with The Element of Water card divination pattern [see p. 118]. This is a good complement to all those themes that have to do with vocation, creativity, endowments, and creative powers. It allows you a great deal of insight into the mirror of your abilities.

General

Navel Chakra (Manipura Chakra)
Will, Power, Control

Object of This Card Divination
With this card divination pattern you learn more about your Naval Chakra. The name Manipura comes from the Sanskrit and can be translated as "shining jewels" or "filled with gems." This name suggests the life energy that is reserved here and then distributed throughout the entire energy system. Your Navel Chakra is the third main chakra; themes such as will, power, protection, feelings, and identity are ascribed to it.

Base

Getting into the Right Mood
Location: above the navel, stomach area; colors: yellow, golden yellow; element: fire; symbol: triangle; planet: Mars

Physical sphere of influence: stomach, gallbladder, liver, spleen, small intestine, the vegetative nervous system, pancreas, abdominal cavity

Healthy flow of energy: the "I" feeling, ability to assert oneself, spontaneity, perseverance, patience, spine, compassion, healthy intuition, dissociation, and protection

Physical disturbances of energy: stomachaches, nervous diseases, diabetes, eating disorders, excess weight, arthritis; diseases of the stomach, gallbladder, liver, pancreas, and spleen; digestive problems

Companion

Emotional energy disturbances: fear of authority, insecurity, nightmares, rage, emotional frigidity, egocentrism, megalomania, inconsiderateness, impatience, aggression, depression, exaggerated ambition, envy, greed, unrest, defenselessness, energy loss

Here are some questions for attuning yourself: What is the outlook with your strength and your power? How do you handle power? What are you employing your will for? How strong is your life energy? Does this area feel powerful or weak? Do you listen to your gut feelings? When can you be manipulated? Concentrate for five to ten minutes on your Sacral Chakra. Which themes can you find for yourself here? Feel inside yourself. You may want to take a few notes. After you have chosen your card decks, begin with laying them out.

Master

Card Divination Pattern
General (Foundation)
1. My Navel Chakra
2. Flow of energy
3. Blockage of energy
4. What do I absorb within me without checking it?
5. My protection

Companion (Support)
6. What is helping me

Master (Apprenticeship)
7. This force protects me

Joker

Joker (*Surprise*)

    8. What supports me and heals me

Tip/Advice

In order to strengthen and to support this chakra, you may also work with the Protection and Strength [see p. 284] or The Element of Fire [see p. 122] card divination patterns.

Heart Chakra (Anahata Chakra)

Love, Compassion, Humanity

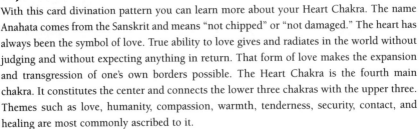

Object of This Card Divination

With this card divination pattern you can learn more about your Heart Chakra. The name Anahata comes from the Sanskrit and means "not chipped" or "not damaged." The heart has always been the symbol of love. True ability to love gives and radiates in the world without judging and without expecting anything in return. That form of love makes the expansion and transgression of one's own borders possible. The Heart Chakra is the fourth main chakra. It constitutes the center and connects the lower three chakras with the upper three. Themes such as love, humanity, compassion, warmth, tenderness, security, contact, and healing are most commonly ascribed to it.

Getting into the Right Mood

Location: the center of the chest, at heart level; colors: green, pink; element: ether; symbol: Solomon's seal; planet: Jupiter

Physical sphere of influence: heart, lungs, thorax, hands, arms, bronchi, circulation, blood, skin, upper back, esophagus

Healthy flow of energy: warmth, charity, openness, healthy dissociation, compassion, tolerance, esteem, attentiveness, group consciousness, environmental consciousness, self-esteem, gratitude, blessing, artistic expressiveness, understanding, trust, cheerfulness, easiness

Physical disturbances of energy: heart problems of all kinds, heart attack, high blood pressure, low blood pressure, illnesses of the lungs and bronchi, shortness of breath, cold, pains in the vertebral column and throughout the back, tenseness in the shoulders

Emotional disturbances of energy: isolation, frigidity, loneliness, hostility, contact difficulties, unkindness, hardness, embitterment, arrogance, too strong or weak dissociation

Here are some questions for attuning yourself: How is your ability to love? How do you keep closeness and distance? Can you allow closeness? Can you dissociate yourself? Can you listen with your heart? Concentrate for five to ten minutes on your Heart Chakra. Which themes can you find here within you? You may wish to take some notes. As soon as you have chosen your card decks, begin laying out your cards.

Card Divination Pattern

General (Foundation)

1. My Heart Chakra
2. My strong points
3. My weak points
4. My relation to myself
5. My relation to others, to the community
6. This I should change or foster

Companion (Support)
7. This force accompanies and guards the strength of my heart
8. This force helps me with blockages

Master (Apprenticeship)
9. This force helps me to develop my ability to love

Joker (Surprise)
10. Which force is helping me and healing me now?

Tip/Advice

This card divination pattern is a good companion for all patterns that have to do with relations of the heart. It affords you a glance into the mirror of your heart's forces.

General

Neck Chakra (Vishuddha Chakra)

Union, Exchange, Communication

Object of This Card Divination

With this card divination pattern you can learn more about your Neck Chakra. The name Vishuddha comes from the Sanskrit meaning "cleansing." The Neck Chakra is the sixth main chakra of our energy system; it constitutes the center of tune and sound. Tunes and sounds can harmonize and purify the atmosphere and even heal. Discordant notes and dissonance, on the other hand, can create illness and other physical disharmony. The Neck Chakra is the center of expression and impression. It connects the center of the heart with the center of the head and mediates between thinking and feeling. It is usually paired with ideas such as union, exchange, communication, mental energy, consciousness of words, independence, justice, expressiveness, and truth.

Base

Getting into the Right Mood

Location: laryngopharynx, cervical vertebral column; colors: turquoise, blue; element: air; symbol: circle; planet: Mercury

Physical sphere of influence: neck, thyroid gland, parathyroid, larynx, voice, jaw, esophagus, windpipe, tonsils, vertebral column, neck, hearing, shoulders, respiration

Healthy flow of energy: clarity, musicality, powers of discernment, ability to learn and concentrate, versatile interests, security, wisdom, harmonizing and healing power, ability to unite, exchange, and develop, power of deduction, expressiveness

Physical disturbances of energy: sore throat and throat problems of all kinds, tonsillitis, dental diseases, neck and shoulder pains, thyroid problems, ear problems, speech impediments

Emotional disturbances of energy: inhibitions, stuttering, lack of communicative power and expressiveness, shyness, isolation, chattiness, striving for power, escape from reality, exaggerated intellect, intolerance, belligerence, striving for fame

Here are some questions for attuning yourself: What do your exchanges with the environment look like? Are you able to make yourself understood? Are you capable of living out your convictions? Are you able to listen? Are you able to create healing images with your words? What do you contribute to the world with your words? Is your Neck Chakra powerful or weak? Concentrate for five to ten minutes on your Neck Chakra. Which themes can you find here within you? You may wish to take some notes. After you have chosen your card decks, you may begin laying out your cards.

Companion

Master

Joker

Card Divination Pattern

Base (Elemental power)

    1. This natural force is working particularly strongly here

General (Foundation)

    2. My Neck Chakra

3. Flow of energy
4. Blockages of energy
5. This is hidden here
6. This I should change or foster

Companion (Support)

7. This force fosters me in this area
8. This force helps me with blockages

Master (Apprenticeship)

9. The power in my Neck Chakra stands under this energy

Joker (Surprise)

10. This strengthens and heals me

Tip/Advice

If you wish to grant this theme even further depth, you may want to work with The Element of Air card divination pattern [see p. 116].

General

Brow Chakra (Anja Chakra)

Direct Perception, Wisdom, Inner Vision

Object of This Card Divination

With this card divination pattern you can learn more about your Brow Chakra. The name Anja comes from the Sanskrit meaning "knowing" or "perceiving." In this center, higher recognitions are possible; also, inner vision opens and the world of the spirit reveals itself. The Brow Chakra is the sixth main chakra and with it the connection to the spiritual world begins. Themes of this area are higher perception, higher realities, psychic abilities, inner vision, third eye, wisdom, truth, freedom, and unity.

Base

Getting into the Right Mood

Location: in the middle of the forehead, between the eyebrows, above the bridge of the nose; colors: indigo, violet; element: ether; symbol: egg; planet: Uranus

Physical sphere of influence: forehead, face, eyes, ears, nose, nervous system, hormone control, pituitary gland, sinus, cerebellum

Healthy flow of energy: openness, faith, trust in self- guidance, imaginative ability, illumination, inner vision, inner reflection, higher knowledge, wisdom, soul bonding, healing power, sensitivity and tactfulness, inner guidance, vastness, ideals, development of higher abilities (e.g., wordless communication, remote viewing, inner journeys, development of the inner senses)

Companion

Physical disturbances of energy: visual impairment, hearing impairment, sinusitis, nervous disorders

Emotional disturbances of energy: flood of thoughts, delusions, hallucinations, self-glorification, superstition, mental confusion, madness, anxieties, senselessness

Here are some questions for attuning oneself: How does your ability to believe in something look? How is your connection to the spiritual realms and to other dimensions? What is your sense of life? What are your ideals? What is your mission? Why are you here? What do you perceive with your inner sight? Concentrate for five to ten minutes on your Brow Chakra. Which themes can you find here with you? You may wish to take a few notes. After you have chosen some card decks, begin laying out your cards.

Master

Card Divination Pattern

General (Foundation)
- 1. My Brow Chakra
- 2. This will open my inner sight
- 3. This blocks my inner sight
- 4. This lies hidden here
- 5. This I should change or foster

Companion (Support)

Joker

- 6. This force accompanies me in this area
- 7. This force helps me with my blockages

Master (Apprenticeship)

    8. This force guides me

Joker (Surprise)

    9. This force strengthens and heals my connection to the worlds of the spirit

Tip/Advice

If you wish to go into this area more intensively, you may want to work with The Principle of Spirituality card divination pattern [see p. 256].

General

Crown Chakra (Sahasrara Chakra)

Peace, Consciousness, Spiritual Guidance

Object of This Card Divination

With this card divination pattern you can learn more about your Crown Chakra. The name Sahasrara comes from the Sanskrit meaning "thousand" or "thousandfold"; therefore, a common symbol for the Crown Chakra is the thousand-leaf lotus flower. As a symbolic number, 1000 reflects perfection, consummation, and eternal union. The Crown Chakra is the seventh main chakra and is considered the gateway to one's pure consciousness.

Base

Common themes of this area are transcendence, cosmic consciousness, mysticism, experience beyond one's senses, redemption, ascent, boundlessness, ecstasy, bliss, self-realization, spirituality, unity

Getting into the Right Mood

Location: zenith of the head, top of the skull, skullcap; colors: gold, white; symbol: lotus; planet: Neptune

Healthy flow of energy: attachment to the cosmos, spiritual strength, all-encompassing knowledge, religiosity, ability to be happy, self-realization, spirituality, mystic experiences, bliss, ecstasy, tranquility, contentment, inspiration, guidance

Companion

Physical disturbances of energy: mental illnesses, life-threatening diseases, cancer, multiple sclerosis, paralysis, headaches, chronic diseases, difficulty in breathing, immune-system weaknesses

Emotional disturbances of energy: confusion, depression, emotional exhaustion, inability to make decisions, lack of high spirits, black magic, superstition, dissolution of self, disinterest in worldly existence, life of seclusion, no rhythm

Occupy yourself with your Crown Chakra. Are you on the verge of realizing your higher self? Have you already had experiences with the spiritual force? Do you know states of tranquility, of deep peace, of happiness, of ecstasy? Have you already had contact with a reality that lies beyond thinking? Concentrate for five to ten minutes on your Crown Chakra. Which themes can you find here within you? You may wish to take some notes. When you have chosen your card decks, begin laying them out.

Master

Card Divination Pattern

General (Foundation)

    1. My Crown Chakra

    2. Flow of energy

    3. Blockages to that energy

    4. This needs to be observed

Joker

    5. This is currently my ideal/my higher aim

Companion (Support)

    6. This force stands by my side here

    7. This force helps me to open up the thousand-leaf lotus flower

Master (*Apprenticeship*)

    8. This force from the spiritual realm is now working

Joker (*Surprise*)

    9. This helps me, supports me, and opens the gate to the spiritual realms

Tip/Advice

In order to grant this theme more depth, you may want to work with the card divination patterns in the Hermetic Principles chapter [see pp. 256–269].

General

The Five Elements—
The Western Tradition

Object of This Card Divination

We all consist of the five elements: fire, earth, water, air, and ether; the latter embodies the quintessence, the core of one's being. With this spread, you can learn how the elements within you are balanced out. You receive a map that represents an inventory of your energy and power system.

Base

Getting into the Right Mood

Before you begin laying out your cards, concentrate upon the five elements. Where do they work in your body and in your life? Which element seems to dominate you? With which element do you appear to have difficulties? In which element do you feel comfortable? First, attune yourself to the respective element and then draw three cards each for this element.

Card Divination Pattern

General (Foundation)

Companion

1. Air: Air streams through your lungs. It ensures constant energy exchange. Air regulates the exchange of information. Air is mental faculty, power of thought, mental power
   1.1. The basic energy inherent in my thinking, within my element of air
   1.2. What fosters or hinders my mental power?
   1.3. What do I need to pay attention to?
2. Water: Eighty to 90 percent of your body consists of water. The body fluids circulate in your body. Water is responsible for transport, supply, and cleansing. Water is sensation, feeling, and ability to love.

Master

   2.1. The basic energy inherent in my emotions, within my element of water
   2.2. What fosters or hinders my emotional power?
   2.3. What do I need to pay attention to?
3. Fire: The inner fire takes care of the burning and the right temperature in the body. Fire is responsible for transformation, warmth, and energy. Fire is force, power, transformation, will.
   3.1. The basic energy inherent in my element of fire
   3.2. What fosters or hinders my power?
   3.3. What do I need to pay attention to?

Joker

4. Earth: The earth gives the soul a temple, a home. The earth is responsible for the rhythm, for the production of talents, for development, and for decay. Earth is matter, body, supply, preservation, and dissolution.

4.1. The basic energy inherent in my body, within my element of earth

4.2. What fosters or prevents my corporeality, my material expressiveness?

4.3. What do I need to pay attention to?

Companion (Support) and Master (Apprenticeship):

5. Ether: Ether is the quintessence that penetrates and vitalizes everything. Ether is oscillation, tone, color, form.

5.1. The crown, the core of my being

5.2. What accompanies me on the inside?

5.3. What accompanies me on the outside?

Tip/Advice

If you wish to work more intensively with an element, then you can do so with the following card divination patterns. If you wish to continue working with the individual elements, you should make a short note about the outcome of this spread, as you can build other patterns upon this foundation.

General

The Five Elements—
The Eastern Tradition

Object of This Card Divination

With the help of this card divination pattern, you can come to recognize and be familiar with the five elements according to Eastern tradition.

Getting into the Right Mood

Base

> *"The sages combined water, fire, wood, metal, and earth, and they held them as inseparable and constant." (Eastern wisdom)*

The Chinese developed their teachings of the elements from the cycles and transforming phases of nature that they observed. The five elements of Eastern tradition are symbols reflecting these processes: wood is growing, elastic, rooted, and strong; fire is dry, hot, ascending, and moving; earth is productive, fertile, and full of seeds; metal is cutting, hard, conductive; water is wet, cool, descending, flowing, and yielding.

Depending on how the elements meet with one another, they either work more or less favorably, as they are mutually conditional and influential. They build upon one another or weaken one another. No single element is more important than another. Each element has counterparts on various levels and is ascribed to various things. It is a very old system that, through Feng Shui, has never lost its significance in countries with ancient Chinese tradition. It is still filled with life and has become quite popular here in the West as well. Whenever we are observing property, a house, a space, or a room, we are, consciously or not, taking in the existing elements such as material, form, pattern, and color. We feel whether the mixture is balanced or whether an element dominates or is lacking.

Companion

Look around your rooms. What color and forms dominate? What kinds of material surround you? What emotions and themes tend to be a little weaker or, on the other hand, which are strong and distinct? Which element is strong in you, and which is weak? Does the environment you created support your dispositions and abilities, or does it seem to oppress you? Does it have a balancing effect on you? How does the distribution of the elements affect the Chi, the life energy, in your rooms and you? Let your environment have an effect on you and listen to your gut feelings. Attune yourself to the subject; to the room, the house, the property, to you, to someone else. Concentrate for a few minutes on it. Let it work within you, and then begin laying out the cards.

Master

Card Divination Pattern

Joker

Base (Elemental power)
    1. Which natural force or which element predominates?
    2. Which natural force or which element is weak?
General (Foundation)
    3. The central topic

4. Wood: flow of energy or blockage?
5. Fire: flow of energy or blockage?
6. Earth: flow of energy or blockage?
7. Metal: flow of energy or blockage?
8. Water: flow of energy or blockage?
9. The Chi, life energy: flow of energy or blockage?
10. Yin/female: flow of energy or blockage?
11. Yang/male: flow of energy or blockage?

Companion (Support)
12. Which force helps me to produce a balance?
13. Which force can I call upon for support?
14. Which force acts through me?

Master (Apprenticeship)
15. The Tai Chi/the life energy of the central theme

Joker (Surprise)
16. This is the source, the origin
17. This is the medicine
18. This is the solution

Tip/Advice

In the event of blockages, draw another card with the question: What needs to be done in order to overcome this obstacle? If you have done what the card advises you to do, then draw another card at a later point with the question: Is the force now balanced? You may also use card divination patterns for the individual elements involved.

The Element of Ether
(Western Tradition)

Object of This Card Divination

With this card divination pattern, you can learn more about your cosmic power; your quintessence, the core of your being, the nature of your inner state, your guidance; simply put, this deals with those forces that support you.

Getting into the Right Mood

Ether is one of the five elements of the Western tradition. From among them it takes on a leading role, for it is the Tai Chi of the West, the Idea, the quintessence that saturates everything and sustains all with life energy. Ether permeates each cell and each atom in the universe.

What kind of relationship do you have with the Higher Self, other dimensions, the cosmos, God—in other words, with the energy penetrating anything? Do you think about the sense of life? What relation do you have with life and with death? Are there events in your life when you have experienced the different force and power of another dimension? When and where have you felt the guidance and providence of the cosmos in your life? What colors do you like in particular? Which sounds, tunes, and music appeal to you? Which fragrances do you like in particular? Which flowers and which stones? What is your relationship to nature? What is your relationship with meadows, trees, creeks, or with the ocean and the mountains, and with animals and people? How is your personal oscillation? Do you feel connected with other dimensions, or are they inaccessible to you? To what extent do you open up to life or to the divine worlds? Are you a religious being? It is from this point that the cosmos flows within you. From here, your power, support, and strength emerge. Attune yourself to the help from above. Then begin laying out cards.

Card Divination Pattern

Base (Elemental power)
1. This natural force works within me.

General (Foundation)
2. The character of the element of ether within me
3. What fosters/blocks the power of ether?
4. My inner state
5. My emotional sound
6. My emotional pattern

Companion (Support)
7. What protects me and accompanies me
8. Which force acts through me
9. Which force helps to get my life energy flowing, to balance it out

Master (Apprenticeship)
10. Under this star/guidance do I stand

Joker (Surprise)

11. The sign: Providence and guidance
12. My medicine: What is healing and supporting me at this moment
13. My energy: What I give to the world through my life energy

Tip/Advice

In this instance, it would be a good idea to work with at least two special card decks (with Master, Joker, Companion, for example, goddesses, angels, etc.).

The Element of Air

(Western and Eastern Traditions)

Object of This Card Divination

With the help of this card divination pattern, you can learn more about the element of air, and about your spiritual abilities and blockages. The Sword in Tarot is associated to the element of air.

Getting into the Right Mood

Base

In the Western tradition, air is considered one of the five elements. Air is associated with the East, as well as with wisdom and knowledge. It is the carrier of information and communication. Its colors are yellow, gold, and white; its planet is Jupiter, its symbol is the sword of clear distinction. As we consist of the elements, air is a part of us as well.

Companion

Close your eyes and concentrate for a few minutes on the air, and how it streams in and out. Feel the lightness of the fresh breeze that it brings with it; how it supplies us with oxygen; how it carries away the old and brings in the new. How is your relationship with the air? How is your respiration; are you breathing deeply and evenly? How is your exchange with the world? In what kind of state is your thought process? Are your thoughts like scampering monkeys? Are you centered and concentrated within you? With what thoughts do you occupy yourself during the day? Do you dominate your power of thought, or does it dominate you? Take some time for yourself; perhaps take a slip of paper and a pen, and write down what comes to mind regarding the element of air. Then begin laying out your cards.

Card Divination Pattern

Base (Elemental power)

    1. This natural force works within me

Master

General (Foundation)

    2. The nature of the element of air within me

    3. The exchange

    4. My communication

    5. My relationship with the world

Companion (Support)

    6. That which heals my air power, protects it and accompanies it

    7. Which force helps me to bring the air within me into balance

Master (Apprenticeship)

    8. Under this star this element stands with me

Joker

Joker (Surprise)

    9. My hidden knowledge

    10. What supports my air and heals it

    11. What I give into the world through my air power

Tip/Advice

If you wish to modify this card divination pattern, one possibility consists in that you first lay out everything with one card deck and then lay out a second round with different decks in order to acquire a deeper insight into the nature of your relationship to the element of air. If there are disturbances, you may work with The Grail Cup card divination pattern [see p. 128].

The Element of Water

(Western and Eastern Traditions)

General

Object of This Card Divination

With the help of this card divination pattern, you can learn more about the element of water within you. It reveals your emotional power and sensation, your strong and weak points in relation to this element, and if there are weak points, how they can be healed. In tarot, the Cup is associated with the element of water.

Base

Getting into the Right Mood

Water is one of the five elements of both the Western and Eastern traditions. In the Eastern tradition water is nurtured by metal; metal is considered an energy supplier and enriches the water. Water has, on the other hand, some control over fire. Water's energy is flowing. Its shape is wavy and irregular; its color is blue-black; the emotions usually associated with it are mildness and fear; the theme in the relationship is knowledge, wisdom, and contact; the direction is North; the plant shape is wavy; the planet is Mercury. That which the water fosters is ascribed to metal and to the colors white, black, or blue. That which the water weakens belongs to the earth and to the colors red and yellow.

Companion

The Western tradition deviates in some points from the Eastern one: in this context, water is ascribed to the West and to twilight; the force of water is flowing, but also magnetic, drawing things toward the bottom. The planet of water is the moon. The colors are blue, turquoise, silver, and gray. The symbol of water in tarot is the Healing Cup.

As we consist of the elements, water is also part of us. Eighty to ninety percent of a human being consists of water. It circulates both in the small cycles in the body and in the great cycles of the earth. Water is flowing energy. Water is movement, supply, cleansing, and healing.

Master

Take a few minutes and observe you inner waters. Water flows as different body fluids throughout your body. How is your relation to water? Is there an inner spring, or do you sometimes feel overwhelmed by the floods of life? What do you think about your emotions and sensations? Are you a person who empathizes, who feels within oneself, and senses how a situation feels? Do you listen to your intuition? Do you listen to your feelings? Which feelings prevail within you? Take your time and perhaps take a slip of paper and a pen and write down what comes to your mind in terms of water. Then begin laying out your cards.

Card Divination Pattern

Joker

Base (Elemental power)
   1. This natural force works within me
General (Foundation)
   2. The nature of my water element
   3. This lies hidden within the depth of my feelings

4. This is what I reveal to the world
5. My flowing force

Companion (Support)

6. This heals, protects, and accompanies the element of water within me
7. This force helps me to bring the water within me into balance

Master (Apprenticeship)

8. Under this star the element stands with me

Joker (Surprise)

9. My sensation
10. This supports and heals the element of water within me
11. This is what I give through my water power into the world

Tip/Advice

A possibility for modifying this card divination pattern consists in first laying out everything with one tarot deck and then laying out a second round with various decks in order to gain a deeper insight into the nature of your relationship with water. If there are disturbances, you may work with The Grail Cup card divination pattern [see p. 128].

The Element of Earth

General

Object of This Card Divination

With the help of this card divination pattern, you can learn more about the element of earth within you. What this means is that you can learn about your physical and material orientations, your talents, your ability to deal with matter, your strong points and weaknesses in terms of this element. In tarot, the Coins symbolize the element of earth.

Base

Getting into the Right Mood

The earth is one of the five elements in both the Western and Eastern traditions. In the Eastern tradition, the earth is nurtured by fire. Fire produces ash, and the earth controls the water: Dikes and given courses in nature restrict the flow of water. The energy of the earth descends and collects; its shape is flat, its color yellow, and its emotions are rest and care; the themes within relationship are giving and taking as well as sincerity; the direction is the middle; the plant shape hangs downward; its planet is Saturn. That which strengthens this element is ascribed to fire, and the colors are green, black, and brown. With earth, the Western tradition deviates in some points from that of the Eastern one: Here the earth is ascribed to the north and to darkness. The force of the earth is centering, leading toward the middle. Its colors are green, brown, and all earth tones. Its symbols are the pentacle (also pentagram) in tarot: the Coins, reflecting the talents/endowments of the power of honoring silence.

Companion

As we consist of the elements, the earth is also a part of us. Earth is substance. It is the ground beneath our feet. The earth is a place of harmony, of richness, and of wealth. Everything originates from it and returns to it.

Ask yourself: What relationship do you have with the earth? What relation do you have to your body? Are you standing with both feet on the ground? Are you at home in richness or in deficiency? How much responsibility have you taken for your life? Are you caring for yourself and perhaps even for others? What does your foundation look like? Are you making use of your talents and abilities; do you bring them to earth? Are you taking care of your living? What relationship do you have with money? How about recurrent activities? Do you enjoy your work? Are you following your calling; are you living your talents and therefore your destiny? How about your rhythm; do you know it; are you living in the rhythm of your nature, are you in harmony with it? Do you have your life under control? Take some time for yourself, and you may wish to take a slip of paper and a pen, and then write down what comes to your mind regarding the theme of earth. Attune yourself to this element and then begin laying out the cards.

Master

Joker

Card Divination Pattern

Base (Elemental power)

1. This natural force within me

General (Foundation)

2. Nature of the element of earth within me (my roots)
3. My strong points, talents, and abilities
4. My richness
5. My being down-to-earth, my stability
6. This I bring into shape

Companion (Support)

7. This protects and accompanies my earth force
8. This helps me to bring my element of earth into balance

Master (Apprenticeship)

9. Under this star the element of earth stands with me

Joker (Surprise)

10. My inner/hidden treasure
11. What heals me and supports me
12. What I give through the element of earth into the world

Tip/Advice

A possibility for modifying this card divination pattern consists in first laying out everything with a tarot deck and then laying out a second round with various decks in order to acquire a deeper insight into the nature of your relationship to the earth. If there are disturbances, you may work with The Grail Cup card divination pattern [see p. 128].

The Element of Fire

(Western and Eastern Traditions)

General

Object of This Card Divination

With the help of this card divination pattern, you can learn more about the element of fire within you. You may convert your power, your wishes and imaginations into reality; furthermore, your energy strengths and blockages lie in this element; in tarot, this element is associated with the Wands.

Base

Getting into the Right Mood

The element of fire is one of the five elements of both the Western and Eastern traditions. In the Eastern tradition, fire is nurtured by wood, for fire is made from wood. Fire even controls metal, for it can melt and deform it. The energy of fire is active. The shape of fire is pointed, sharp-edged, and triangular; the color ascribed to it is red. Its emotions are joy and hatred; the themes in a relationship are appearance, expressiveness; the direction is south; the form of plant is the blossom; the planet is Mars. However, there is also a star: the sun. That which strengthens this element is ascribed to wood and to the colors green and red. Water, blue, and black weakens the fire. The Western tradition agrees with those points in

Companion

essence. In addition, fire is also ascribed to the south. Its colors are red, orange, garish light green, violet, and black.

As we consist of the elements, fire is also a part of us. Fire is warmth and light, it produces warmth and light. It makes us powerful, blazes up brightly, and drives us on, full of sparkling vitality. To get in touch with fire means to feel its presence.

Before you begin laying out the cards, meditate over the element of fire. What relationship do you have with fire? Is it pleasant or threatening to you? What about your driving force as well as forces of conversion and expressing your desires and ideas? Are you an active or a passive person? What about your sexuality? How is your energy in dealing with

Master

other people? Are you able to stand up for yourself? Do you feel strong or weak? Can you control your energy or does it sometimes break free from within you? What are you using your energy for? How do you direct your energy?

Take some time for yourself; you may wish to take a slip of paper and write down what comes to mind in terms of the theme of fire. Attune yourself to this element and then begin laying out your cards.

Card Divination Pattern

Base (Elemental power)
    1. This natural force works within me
General (Foundation)

Joker

    2. Nature of the element of fire within me
    3. My strong points
    4. My weak points

5. My driving force, my engine

Companion (Support)

6. This protects and accompanies the element of fire within me

7. This force helps me to bring the fire within me into balance

Master (Apprenticeship)

8. Under this star this element stands with me

Joker (Surprise)

9. My power

10. This supports and heals the fire in me

11. This I send out into the world through the element of fire

Tip/Advice

One possibility for modifying this card divination pattern consists in first laying out everything with only one card deck (e.g., a tarot deck) and then laying out a second round with other decks in order to gain a deeper insight into the nature of your relation to the element of fire. If there are disturbances, you may work with The Grail Cup card divination pattern [see p. 128].

The Element of Wood

(Eastern Tradition)

General

Object of This Card Divination

With this card divination pattern, you can have a good look at the element of wood from the elemental teachings according to the Eastern tradition.

Getting into the Right Mood

Base

The element of wood is nurtured by water, just as a tree needs water for its growth. Wood dominates the earth, for a tree absorbs nutrients from the earth. The energy of the wood is directed upward and sideward: It is expansive. The shape ascribed to the wood is high, soaring, and cylindrical. Its color is green; and its emotions are kindness, anger, and rage. The themes in a relationship are flexibility and receptiveness; the direction in the room is to the east; the shape of the plant is soaring; the planet is Jupiter. That which strengthens this element is ascribed to water and is green, black, or blue. Metal, white, and yellow weaken this element. As all elements are within us, wood is a part of us.

A tree best conveys the idea of the element of wood: A tree will grow as long as it lives. It absorbs its food from the earth. Water helps it to thrive, to blossom, and to grow. it is a being rooted within the earth striving upward, expanding on the inside and the outside, upward and sideward. A tree carries fruit and the seed of new life in it, through which the cycle renews itself. When a human being is like a tree in the woods, then his or her energy of life is healthy and clear; this being is grounded and thus grows.

Companion

Take a few minutes for yourself. Close your eyes and imagine how you are growing as a tree. Where would you stand? How would your roots be and your crown; how your trunk; how your bark? Would you stand alone or in a group? On which soil would you stand? How would your energy be? Do you feel grounded and rooted? Can you be easily knocked over, brought out of balance? Do you have sufficient sun and food to thrive? Are you growing further in your being or has something brought your growth to a halt? What would foster your growth, what would help you; what would hinder your growth? What about your fruits? What do you absorb from the cycle, what do you give into it? Is wood rather beneficial or obstructive? Do you feel connected with the element of wood? How do you perceive it within you? After you have attuned yourself, begin laying out your cards.

Master

Card Divination Pattern

Base (Elemental power)
    1. This natural force works within me

General (Foundation)
    2. The element of wood within me
    3. My relation to the element of wood
    4. My roots, my standing position
    5. My trunk, my expansion

Joker

6. My crown
7. My growth

Companion (Support)

8. This protects and accompanies the element of wood within me
9. This force helps to bring the element of wood within me into balance

Master (Apprenticeship)

10. Under this star the element of wood stands with me

Joker (Surprise)

11. My force
12. This heals and supports my wood
13. This I give through the element of wood into the world

Tip/Advice

A possible modification to this card divination pattern consists in first laying out all cards down (e.g., with tarot) and then laying out a second round with other decks to acquire a deeper insight into the nature of your relation to wood. If there are disturbances, you may work with The Grail Cup card divination pattern [see p. 128].

The Element of Metal

(Eastern Tradition)

Object of This Card Divination

Through this card divination pattern you can have a good look at the element of metal from the elemental teachings according to the Eastern tradition.

Getting into the Right Mood

Base

The element of metal is one of the five elements of the Eastern tradition. The energy of metal contracts, condenses, and goes inward. Its shape is round and domelike; its color is white. The emotions ascribed to it are bravery and grief; the themes in a relationship are talking/listening, as well as justice; the direction is to the west; the shape of the plant is pointed and needlelike; the planet is Venus. That which strengthens this element belongs to the earth and has the colors yellow and white. That which weakens this element is ascribed to the fire and has the colors green with red.

As we consist of the elements, metal is also a part of us. In the form of the earth's minerals it ensures the richness of the soil and supplies valuable components that let our food grow and enrich it—minerals are the salt of the earth. Metal is the condensation of the earth. It provides the foundation for the solidity of tools and buildings. This is the raw material for the beauty reflected in jewels, precious stones, and minerals. Perseverance, continuance, solidity, value, life preservation, and love give a feeling for the element of metal. Furthermore, metal is one of the main components of today's communication systems. It is the substance of which our wires and our supply networks are made. It creates a connection over far distances and conducts electricity. Metal shows us the strength within our own being.

Companion

Master

Here are some questions for attuning yourself: How does it look with your conductivity? How do you feel connected to yourself and to the world? How about your substance, your inner reserves? Can you refine things, make them more beautiful, and transform them? What does your inner power supply look like? Can you center yourself within you and compose yourself? Attune yourself to the element within you, and then begin laying out your cards.

Card Divination Pattern

Base (Elemental power)

    1. This natural force works within me

General (Foundation)

Joker

    2. The element of metal within me

    3. My relation to the element of metal

    4. Fostering or hindering influences

    5. My strong points

    6. My conductivity/my ability to communicate within and without me

    7. My art/my endowment

Companion (Support)

8. This protects and accompanies the element of metal within me
9. This force helps to bring the element of metal within me into balance

Master (Apprenticeship)

10. Under this star the element of metal stands within me

Joker (Surprise)

11. My reserve
12. This heals and protects me
13. This I give into the world through the element of metal

Tip/Advice

A possible modification of this card divination pattern consists in first laying out all cards with one deck (e.g., tarot) and then laying out a second round with other decks in order to obtain a deeper insight into the nature of your relation to metal. In case there are disturbances, you may want to work with The Grail Cup card divination pattern [see p. 128].

The Grail Cup
The Healing Cup

General

Object of This Card Divination

With this card divination pattern, you can examine your illness or your problem more thoroughly and thus you can learn to understand it. You can even receive hints to what should be changed for a healing process to take place.

Getting into the Right Mood

Base

Before you begin laying out the cards, take some time for yourself. Think about your problem (your illness). When did it start? What was the reason/the trigger? How did the problem reveal itself? On which occasions did it get better, and when did it become worse? What is your share in it? Illnesses are a cry for help by your soul: A negative pattern of thinking and feeling has been acting on you for so long that it finally shows as a physical symptom. Many diseases can be transformed, weakened, and cured through new patterns. Think about which dogma or conviction could possibly be behind your illness. You may wish to take a few notes regarding this theme. Attune yourself to your question, then choose your cards and begin laying them out.

Card Divination Pattern

Companion

General (Foundation)
1. My self-image
2. The problem/the illness
3. What is the cause/reason for my illness?
4. The pattern that needs to be processed
5. The secret, the hidden things, the undiscovered things

Companion (Support)
6. Which force helps and heals me?
7. With which force should I work particularly intensively?

Master

Master (Apprenticeship)
8. Which force stabilizes me?
9. Which new pattern is right for me right at this point?

Joker (Surprise)
10. What is the Healing Cup, or, in other words, the medicine?

Tip/Advice:

Joker

If you wish to occupy yourself even more intensively with the health and healing theme, then you may want to continue working with the card divination patterns in the health chapters The Seven Chakras [pp. 94–109] and The Five Elements [pp.110–127]. If you wish to know if your illness is based on your family structure, then you can work with the Families: The Primal Family card divination pattern [see p. 66].

If you have the feeling that your illness/your problem has to do with your relationship, then the Relationship Analysis card divination pattern [see p.62] may help you further. If you wish to know whether your illness is of karmic origin, then you may work with the Visiting the Karmic Council card divination pattern [see p. 286]. And if you have the inkling that you are being attacked from the outside, then the Energy Vampire [see p. 282] and Ancient Oath [see p. 280] card divination patterns can be of further assistance.

General

Crisis

Understanding and Dissolution

Object of This Card Divination

This card divination pattern will help you to tackle a crisis more intensively, to illuminate it, to understand it, to recognize the themes that are involved in it, and ultimately to transform that understanding into permanent realization.

Getting into the Right Mood

Base

"Change is the only constant." (Buddhist wisdom)

Take some time, silence, and space to think about your current situation; you may light a candle to do so. Listen inside yourself. Ask yourself: When did the crisis start? What triggered it? How long has this crisis been going on? What is the central theme of the crisis; what is it all about? What prevents you from moving on? What do you have to say farewell to for good? What can you take with you? What is now important for your healing? What do you need in order to escape this crisis? If you feel like it, you may take some notes. As soon as you have attuned yourself, choose your cards and begin laying them out.

Card Divination Pattern

Companion

General (Foundation)

    1. This is where I failed

    2. This was previously spared and now helps me

    3. This is the way out

    4. These are the ways and the goals for the near future

Companion (Support)

    5. This force helps me to understand the crisis and thus change it

    6. This force leads out of the crisis

Joker (Surprise)

    7. This force heals the wounds that have arisen through the crisis

Master (Apprenticeship)

    8. Under this star the coming times stand

Master

Tip/Advice:

If you happen to get into a crisis, this is because the time is ripe for you to take another step in your development. Remember that the strength for this step is there. Whether or not you wish to accept the challenge contained within is entirely up to you. You may also work with

Joker

The Grail Cup card divination pattern [see p. 128].

Ideal and Reality

General

Object of This Card Divination

With the help of this card divination pattern, you can observe how the Ideal and the Real stand in relation to one another within you. Through this, you can recognize what is required to bring Ideal and Reality into line. This picture card is suited for all themes that occupy you.

Getting into the Right Mood

Base

"The Way is the goal." (Chinese wisdom)

The Ideal is the engine and Reality is what can be altered, what can develop and change. In order to attune yourself, pose the following questions: What is my current situation? What is my Ideal? What do I wish for myself? What is Reality? How does my life currently look? What needs to be done in order for me to reach my Ideal? What can remain as it is? What needs to be changed? As soon as you have attuned yourself, choose your cards and then begin laying them out.

Card Divination Pattern

Companion

General (Foundation)

    1. The central theme: what it is all about
    2. Conscious aspects
    3. Unconscious aspects
    4. The base/the reality
    5. A deed that supports me on my way
    6. An insight/realization that strengthens me on my way
    7. The goal/the ideal
    8. Anxieties and hopes
    9. Unexpected influences
    10. Outcome of the matter according to the way things stand

Master

Companion (Support)

    11. The accompanying, supporting force

Master (Apprenticeship)

    12. The higher significance

Joker (Surprise)

    13. The gift of the cosmos

Joker

Tip/Advice:

You may deepen your theme with Blind Spot [see p. 134] and the card divination patterns in the Hermetic Principles chapter [se pp. 256–269].

Blind Spot

General

Object of This Card Divination

This card divination pattern is suitable for all themes of life. Here, you may illuminate those aspects that are like blind spots that you have not yet considered in particular or have yet wished to see.

Getting into the Right Mood

Base

The blind spot is that point or aspect which we ourselves are not able to notice or might not wish to notice. It is the dead angle in the rear mirror of your car: It is the piece that is missing to solve a matter, a theme, a situation, even a conflict within or without us with which we attempt to come to terms. This problem area can have a variety of causes. We can, for example, be blind in one spot because our patterns of behavior originate from a very young age, or it might stem from an experience that we have dispelled. It may even lie within our peripheral knowledge of the matter. Before you begin laying out your cards, envision the theme that is currently occupying you as accurately as possible. Here are some questions for attuning yourself: In what position are you? What are you contributing to it? What do others contribute to it? What is known to you but not to others? What is the point at which you are stuck? Have you been in this situation more than once already? Does it belong to your theme of life? Can you recognize a pattern in it? When you have attuned yourself to the topic, choose your cards and then begin laying them out.

Companion

Card Divination Pattern

Base (Elemental power)

    1. The natural force at work: What it is all about

General (Foundation)

    2. Known to the questioner/to others: What everyone knows

Master

    3. Unknown to the questioner/unknown to others: The great unknown; the unconsciously driving force; the ally

    4. Known to the questioner/unknown to others: The hidden thing; that which only the questioner knows

    5. Unknown to the questioner/known to others: That which only others know; the blind spot

Companion (Support)

    6. Support

Joker (Surprise)

    7. Healing

Joker

Tip/Advice:

If you wish to research further at this point, you may work with the card divination patterns in the Hermetic Principles chapter [see pp. 256–269].

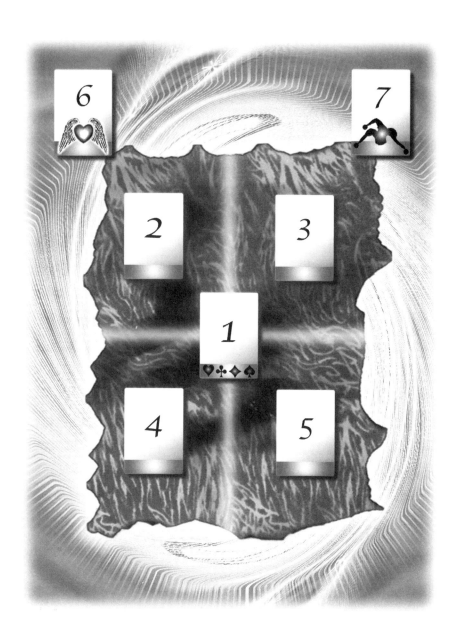

General

Inner and Outer Stages of Change

Object of This Card Divination
This card divination pattern helps you to acquire an inner and outer vision of change.

Getting into the Right Mood
Variation and change are processes. These processes have a beginning, a course, and at some point they reveal themselves in our changed behavior. If, for example, we want to quit smoking, then it is good not to simply eliminate the cigarette alone. We must also work on

Base

our inner attitude so that smoking cannot implant itself permanently in our life and so trigger a relapse after only a short time. If we wish to change an old pattern, it is better to work with it both on the inside and on the outside so that we can develop a new behavior.

Here are some questions for attuning yourself: What would I like to change? Which inner attitude contributes to old things remaining as they are? What is my goal? What is the way to get there? Which inner attitude needs to be newly developed? What steps need to be pursued on the outside? What needs to be observed in my environment? Who is behind me? Who would never support me? What helps me? What are my power sources? Take notes. Write down the advantages and disadvantages of the old pattern and replace the

Companion

advantages with new, similar forms that do not support the old pattern. You may also draw up a plan for how to get from your current position to your goal. When you have become attuned to the theme, choose your cards and then begin laying them out.

Card Divination Pattern
General (Foundation)
1. Central theme
2. The hidden side of the central theme
3. Advantages

Master

4. Disadvantages
5. The inner steps that I need to take
6. What needs to be adjusted
7. What I need to work on
8. The outer steps I need to take
9. What needs to be left alone
10. What needs to be done
11. What I need to observe in particular
12. What hinders/fosters me in this process

Joker

13. What does the future bring?
Base (Elemental power)
14. Which natural force needs to be particularly observed?

Companion (*Support*)

15. Which force supports this undertaking?
16. Which force can I call on in difficult situations?

Master (*Apprenticeship*)

17. What does the higher-level change signify?

Joker (*Surprise*)

18. What helps me with my inner steps?
19. What helps me with my outer steps?
20. Which force helps me in my most difficult phases?

Tip/Advice

In order to gain a greater sense of depth with this theme, you may want to work with The Principle of Correspondence card divination pattern [see p. 258].

Inner Balance

General

Object of This Card Divination

This card divination pattern serves as one's inner reflection. With its help you can ascertain how the forces are distributed within you, and thus you can straighten out imbalances.

Getting into the Right Mood

Our inner balance consists of an active and a passive side; you can feel it. Close your eyes. Concentrate on your body. First get a feel for your right side and then for your left side. Which side is richer in energy? Which side is dominant?

Base

For this card divination pattern, divide your general cards in two stacks. Draw all cards face down first. Feel which stack stands for the passive side and which one for the active side. Now, from the stack determined to be passive, draw two cards for the passive side. Similarly, draw two cards for the active side from the stack that you have chosen as active. Bring the remaining cards together once more into one stack. Then draw two cards from this stack for the head and then two cards for the legs. When you have drawn all the cards, begin laying them out face up.

Companion

Card Divination Pattern

General Cards

  1. Passive side: My self-esteem/how I accept myself
  2. Passive side: I am currently going through this learning process
  3. Active side: How I act on the outside
  4. Active side: My behavior, my action
  5. My head/my mind/my thoughts
  6. Fostering/hindering influences
  7. My stomach/my feeling/my relation to the world
  8. Fostering/hindering influences
  9. My legs/my standing/my grounding
  10. Fostering/hindering influences

Master

Base (Elemental power)

  11. This elemental power/natural force is unbalanced within me
  12. This elemental power/natural force is balanced within me

Companion (Support)

  13. This force helps me to straighten out my inner balance
  14. This force I can call upon when experiencing disturbances

Master (Apprenticeship)

  15. The cosmic council/the higher vision

Joker

Joker (Surprise)

  16. This helps me and brings about my inner balance
  17. The hidden, helpful force that I can activate

The Descent into the Underworld

Object of This Card Divination

With this card divination pattern you can meet your shadow—that which you do not wish to see—to make it a part of yourself and, by doing so, transform a weakness into a strength.

Getting into the Right Mood

> *"Into the blazing flames I lay my heart. Quietly it contracts as if from pain.*
> *But all of a sudden it grasps the penetrating flood, and ripens into a flame*
> *and to eternal fervor."* (Will Vesper)

The underworld is the residence and kingdom of the lower divinities and of fire beings. It is also the home of the deceased. According to most world views, the entrance to the underworld is in the west, for that is where the sun sets, on the other side of the ocean. We can find within all cultures the description of a shadow realm existing here. In the Jewish tradition, it is called Abaddon, in the Greek culture Hades, in the Roman Orcus, in the Germanic Hel, in the Egyptian Duat, and in various native Indian ones Mitnal, Mictlan, Ucu, Pacha, Xibalba, etc. If we wish to look into the mirror of our hidden points, our shadow side, then we must begin our journey into the underworld. For here lies the power of

change, of decay, and, consequently, of rearrangement. After the descent, we will be born anew; we develop new strengths, for we have recognized dark, hidden parts in us, lifted them into light and, thus, redeemed them.

Here are some questions for attuning yourself: On which shadow elements within you have you already worked? What theme do you encounter in your life time and again? What burdens or troubles you? Which dark feelings do you perceive within you? What triggers negative or vehement feelings in you? Where do you still sense unanswered questions? Whom or what have you not yet forgiven? What stirs uneasily inside of you? What encourages you to dare the descent into the underworld? What would you like to recognize, to

name, and to redeem? What would you like to heal at this moment? Let the shadows take shape within you so that you may recognize them. When you have attuned yourself, choose your cards and begin laying them out.

Card Divination Pattern

Base (Elemental power)

    1. Which natural force do I need to particularly observe?

General (Foundation)

    2. The gatekeeper at the entrance of the underworld: What do I need to observe on

       my journey?

    3. The first gate to the underworld

    4. The second gate to the underworld

    5. The third gate to the underworld

    6. The fourth gate to the underworld

7. The fifth gate to the underworld
8. The sixth gate to the underworld
9. The seventh gate to the underworld
10. The shadow side
11. The sacrifice for the underworld
12. The food of life: the first enlivening force
13. The water of life: the second enlivening force
14. The flower of life: the third enlivening force
15. The ascent

Companion (Support)
16. + 17. These helping forces: the allies

Master (Apprenticeship)
18. The side of light: the cosmic guidance
19. The newly rising star

Joker (Surprise)
20. The healing
21. The newly developing force

Tip/Advice

If you choose to work with this card divination pattern, let the message of your cards work upon you for some time. Pay attention to your dreams and to that which surfaces from within you. Take your time. Too often, we would like to quickly push aside the dark side and ignore it; however, by doing so, it is not allowed to dissolve, and so it cannot be redeemed. In order to gain more depth in regards to this theme, you can work with the Blind Spot [see p. 134], The Path through the Middle World [see p. 142], and The Ascent into the Upper World [see p. 144] card divination patterns as well as with the card divination patterns in the Hermetic Principles chapter [see pp. 256–269].

General

The Path through the Middle World

Encounter with the Ruling Forces

Object of This Card Divination

Through this card divination pattern, you can gain an insight into the forces that currently prevail in your life.

Getting into the Right Mood

Base

"All things are connected as in the finest web of a spider. The slightest movement on any thread can be discerned from all points in the web. Start at any point on the web and find that you are at the center. All our lives are locked together in the shimmering web in which all things are enmeshed, and connected to one another. Everything vibrates the web, whether it is an act of the gods or the movement of the tiniest insect" (Brian Bates)

The Middle World is a realm illuminated by thousands of candles. It consists of the immediate perception of the forces acting at the moment, from whatever realms they might come. With our words, we can only differentiate the shadows of Reality, whereas our soul is capable of meeting the Middle World without a veil. The Middle World realm is too complex to fully grasp. We ourselves are part of it and thus cannot step back and observe it. Yet we can

Companion

learn to receive the messages, to interpret the patterns, and to recognize the signs that lie on our path. They nurture us and guide us on our inner path. The forces of the Middle World are like the winds and the tides for a fisherman. He recognizes them, and he can align his sails and his rudder accordingly; in short, he acts in harmony with the forces. The forces of the Middle World protect and warn us; they advise and help us. If we go with them, we will be safely guided.

Here are some questions for attuning yourself: What is your current state of being? Do you have the feeling of progress/that it is difficult/that it is easy/that you are not making any headway? What is your situation at the moment? Which forces do you feel in your life?

Master

How do they express themselves in your life? What is a possible focus of learning? Before you begin laying your cards, you may wish to take a small journey into your inner world. Allow what happens and what meets you, for these are the forces that are working now.

Card Divination Pattern

Base (Elemental power)

    1. This natural force is currently working particularly strongly

General (Foundation)

    2. The preparation: What I need to observe

Joker

    3. The gate to the Middle World: The access

    4. The path: hindering/fostering influences

    5. The purification: What needs to be done

    6. The source: The origin, the force

    7. The reflection: That which reflects

8. The dark forest: That must be considered
9. The force called: This force of mine is activated
10. Rainbow's place: This force can be activated
11. The inner temple: The resting point
12. The secret: that which is hidden
13. The message of inner guidance
14. The place of adventures: what happens next

Companion (Support)

15. Which force is accompanying me now?

Here, you may draw one card from all companion decks that you have and that appeal to you now; observe their overall message and allow them to have an effect on you.

Master (Apprenticeship)

16. The current time stands under this star

Joker (Surprise)

17. The omen/the sign/the hint for this time
18. These forces are presently helpful in difficult situations
19. That is the opportunity for growth/the task of learning for this time

Tip/Advice

If you have runes (cards or stones), then it is recommended that, with this card divination pattern, you draw one rune, for runes are the original signs of the Middle World. In addition, plants, minerals, animals, and messengers of nature are equally suitable as support with this pattern. If you like, you can explore the way through the Middle World even more thoroughly with The Descent into the Underworld [see p. 140] and The Ascent into the Upper World [see p. 144] card divination patterns. By doing so, you can learn which force from these worlds also acts with you now.

General

The Ascent into the Upper World

Meeting with the One's Own Light

Object of This Card Divination

With this card divination pattern, you can learn more about the forces from the Upper World that currently work in your life.

Getting into the Right Mood

Base

The Upper World is the realm of light. From there, cosmic radiance streams toward us and enriches our daily life. We receive the messages of the shining worlds; these messages steer and guide us so we remain on the path we have determined for ourselves. As the stars follow their paths and shape new constellations, so the forces from the Upper World influence our current situations and, as a result, we are provided time and again with new possibilities.

Card Divination Pattern

Base (Elemental power)

    1. This natural force needs to be observed

Companion

General (Foundation)

    2. The threshold: This needs to be observed

    3. What I need to shed: This should be left behind

    4. The ascent

Companion (Support)

    5. The companion into the Upper World

        You may also have several forces accompanying you into the Upper World. Listen closely to your feelings.

Master (Apprenticeship)

Master

    6. The encounter: The message that should now reach me

Joker (Surprise)

    7. The medicine

    8. The council

    9. The force

    10. One's own light

Joker

The I-Am Presence

The Higher Self

General

Object of This Card Divination

With this card divination pattern, you can experience the forces of your I-am presence.

Getting into the Right Mood

"Nobody shall be equal to someone else, yet everybody shall be equal to the highest.
How is this to be done? Quite simple—let everyone perfect him—or herself."
(translated from: Die Gegenwart der Meister)

Base

The teaching of the I-am presence is ancient and originally comes from the mysticism of the Far East. It refers to the higher self of the human being, something on a level with the "Buddha nature," the "Christ force," etc. With each new life, we are given a new opportunity to come closer to the divine force within us. Within our I-am presence is our divine force, our light, that which guides us and that which already works through us.

Here are some questions for attuning yourself: Which color has always been your favorite? Which force do you feel within you when you are balanced in your center? What abilities and characteristics do you have? What do you give into the world? How do others see you? Attune yourself to your higher presence, choose your cards, and then begin laying them out.

Companion

Card Divination Pattern

Base (Elemental power)

    1. Which natural force needs to be particularly observed?

General (Foundation)

    2. Preparation

    3. Energetic (fine material) cleansing

    4. The silver cord/the elevator/the way upward

    5. The seven rays/the seven gates

    6. Blue: power-will

    7. Gold/yellow: wisdom-knowledge

    8. Pink: love-compassion

    9. White: purity-ascent

    10. Green: healing-blessing

    11. Red: peace-active love

    12. Violet: transformation-redemption

    13. The gate to the higher level: This I need to observe

Companion (Support)

    14. The accompanying forces

       Here, you can also draw several accompanying forces from various decks. Listen to your gut feelings.

Master

Joker

15. The force that accompanies me in my everyday life

Master (*Apprenticeship*)

16. The message of my I-am presence
17. The strength that radiates through me into life

Joker (*Surprise*)

18. The coat of protection
19. The won/found/discovered force
20. The healing
21. The implementation in one's daily life

Tip/Advice

If you wish to gain deeper insight into this theme, you may learn more about the forces in your life with The Element of Ether [see p. 114], The Ascent into the Upper World [see p. 144], and The Descent into the Underworld [see p. 140] card divination patterns.

Conception, Pregnancy, Birth

Object of This Card Divination

With this card divination pattern, you can examine the pregnancy and birth stages of life more thoroughly—especially if you are an expecting parent or if you wish to explore what was happening during this period of time back then. The card divination pattern is also suitable for several people (e.g., for a family, for expecting parents, or for a mother and her child).

Getting into the Right Mood

> "Receive with awe, teach through love, release into liberty."
>
> (Rudolf Steiner, 1861-1925)

Conception, pregnancy, and birth are the first three stages a soul traverses as it is born. However, the little soul probably receives its first impressions even before conception and pregnancy. For father and mother each carries particular themes within that do not only complement with those of the partner but also with the theme of life of the coming child. Each person is different, and thus newborns already have their very own personality. When a child is born, he or she manifests the endowments and themes from the family of the mother and from that of the father as well as his or her very own. Getting to know the parents, establishing position in the sibling hierarchy, developing along the course of pregnancy, being born, and living the hour of birth already grant a great deal of information about the endowments and themes that a child will carry through his or her life.

Here are some questions for attuning yourself: How did the parents get to know each other? When did the child kick for the first time? How did the woman/the man behave when this kicking first happened? Which changes take/took place? What preferences or aversions manifested themselves? Are there any particular events that will enter or have already entered into the tales of the family chronicles? Which decisive points, experiences, and themes predominated during the time of pregnancy? Choose your cards and then begin laying them out.

Card Divination Pattern

General (Foundation)

1. The central theme of life
2. The hidden/inner theme of life
3. Conception
4. Pregnancy
5. Birth
6. The paternal dispositions
7. The maternal dispositions
8. + 9. One's own dispositions and abilities
10. What needs to be observed

Base (Elemental power)
11. The natural force that accompanies the child
12. The power of destiny

Companion (Support)
13. The help
14. The force that stands by one's side in difficult situations

Master (Apprenticeship)
15. The star under which life stands

Joker (Surprise)
16. The miracle/the unexpected assistance
17. The reserve that can be activated when needed

Tip/Advice

When disturbances or deviating courses appear, you can work with the Special Questions about Individual Stages card divination patterns [see p. 174]. You may examine unclear or ominous cards more thoroughly with Clarifying Ambiguous Cards [see p. 44]. In addition, you may use the Expecting Parents card divination pattern [see p. 184] to give some depth to the theme. In addition, The Inner Child [see p. 72] is suitable for personal work during this time, and, with Destiny of Life [see p. 186] you may observe this theme more closely.

General

Birth to Age 7

From Infant to Toddler-Age of Imitation

Object of This Card Divination

With this card divination pattern you can, at any time, examine this particular phase of your own childhood or of any child currently at this stage of life.

Getting into the Right Mood

"Let the soul of children grow, give it the hand into the unknown land."

Base

In the first seven-year stage, the development of a child leaps ahead more quickly than at any other time later on. A human being is born and sees the light of this world. The child learns to straighten up, to walk, to talk, to express him- or herself, and to develop a proper personality: the "I" ability. The child slowly begins to discover the spaces of life, to expand spheres of activity, and to explore his or her small environment in a creative manner. The dependence on the family and the influence of the nurturing person in the small world of the child is at present at its greatest. The sky is still open, and the child is a wanderer between worlds. At this stage, the power of the heart is formed. Conscious and unconscious behavioral patterns are acquired, separate from those the person has already brought into the world in the forms of endowments, characteristics, and abilities. In this phase, the foundation for one's future life is established. Here, personal themes are revealed as well as those arising from the closer surroundings of the child. The family is the smallest unit in society. As it is on a small scale thus it is also on a large scale. The way the child experiences his or her own being within the small world of the family will also be the manner in which the child will experience his or her own being in the outside world.

Companion

Here are some questions for attuning yourself: How does/did this first stage of life pass? What endowments, characteristics, and particularities have been brought along? Where is parental behavior reflected in the behavior of the child or in my own? Is/was this stage of life harmonious or were there setbacks? Which particularities seem to constitute this part of life? Choose your cards and then begin laying them out.

Master

Card Divination Pattern

General (Foundation)
1. Central theme of the birth to age 7 stage
2. The base/the roots/the family

3. + 4. Flow of energy/disturbance of energy
5. Inner endowments

Joker

6. Influence from the outside
7. What needs to observed/to be fostered right now?

Base (Elemental power)
8. Which element needs to be particularly observed?

Companion (Support)

    9. Which force accompanies this time?

    10. Which force will stand by the child's side in difficult situations?

Master (Apprenticeship)

    11. Under which star does/did this time stand?

Joker (Surprise)

    12. This is helping and supporting me, and healing this stage right now?

Tip/Advice

With disturbances or deviating courses, you may work here with the Special Questions about Individual Stages card divination pattern [see p. 174]. If you wish to gain still more knowledge in regard to this phase, you may do so with the Destiny of Life spread [see p. 186]; also, the spread Exerting Influence on Unfavorable Developments [see p. 174] can assist you even further.

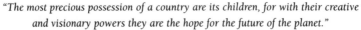

8 to 14 Years of Age

Childhood and School Days

Object of This Card Divination

With this card divination pattern you can, at any time, examine this particular phase of your childhood or the time of a child who is currently at this stage of life.

Getting into the Right Mood

> *"The most precious possession of a country are its children, for with their creative and visionary powers they are the hope for the future of the planet."*

Base

In the second seven-year stage, the first great separation from the home and the close surroundings takes place: school days begin. Friends, teachers, and other educators begin to influence the child. The much larger surrounding plays a bigger role from now on. The child now trains the powers of the mind. Furthermore, social behavior is acquired and sharpened in this phase. The child begins to question, wanting to know everything and beginning to wonder about life. Talents, endowments, abilities, and characteristics are now clearly visible. Moreover, the child recognizes him- or herself within the larger context of the world, and many illusions of the infant stage break. The reliability of experience and delivered knowledge is tested.

Companion

Here are some questions for attuning yourself: How does/did this second stage of life pass? Which forces develop? How are they dealt with? What other people have exerted influence on the child? How did they affect the child? Is/was this stage of life harmonious or were there setbacks? What insights are/were gained? How is/was the adult world perceived? Which particularities determine this stage of life? Choose the cards and begin laying them out.

Card Divination Pattern

Master

General (Foundation)

1. Central theme of the stage from 8 to 14 years of age
2. Roots/parental home—fostering/hindering influences?
3. School days—fostering/hindering influences?
4. Friendship—fostering/hindering influences?

5. + 6. What can be left as it is, and what needs to go?

7. What should be observed/fostered?
8. Chance of growth?

Base (Elemental power)

9. Which element should be given attention?

Joker

Companion (Support)

10. Which force accompanies this time?
11. Which force stands/stood by the child's side in difficult situations?

Master (Apprenticeship)

    12. Under which star does/did this time stand?

Joker (Surprise)

    13. What is supporting and healing this stage now?

    14. What is helping now in difficult situations?

Tip/Advice

With disturbances or deviating courses, you may want to work with the Special Questions about Individual Stages card divination pattern [see p. 174]. If you would like to deepen the themes in this stage of life, you many continue with both the Principle of Correspondence [see p. 258] and The Inner Child [see p. 72] card divination patterns.

15 to 21 Years of Age

Adolescence, Puberty

General

Object of This Card Divination

With this card divination pattern you can, at any time, examine this particular phase of your youth or the time of a youngster who is currently at this stage of life.

Getting into the Right Mood

Base

"Don't look into the eyes of that one human being in order to reflect yourself in them, but look for friends with whom you look out into the world. Discover the world." (Anonymous)

The third seven-year stage begins the great breaking off from the nuclear home. The school days have marched on. The human being has already established his or her social surroundings. However, the other people to whom the adolescent relates must be counted in as well. The youth also reaches that time when his or her sex and gender begin to have a significant impact. The young person develops into a mature young woman or young man. The opposite sex becomes important, and people begin to choose partners. Often the first blow of lovesickness clouds the heart. The question regarding the sense of life stands in the foreground, and people say farewell to their childhood. The individual crosses a threshold at this stage. The person makes the painful discovery that many things that were done in earlier times are now no longer possible (e.g., singing, dancing, frolicking, and cuddling with the parents). The person feels stiff, awkward, and insecure within his or her body and, subsequently, the body must be rediscovered as must the sense of the inner self. On the other hand, he or she also begins to discover the world. The adolescent develops dreams, desires, hopes, and ideals. The gate into the world opens up. Here, one begins to develop an inkling of the course for the future. The individual goes through his or her first moon knot; this means that the relationship that the moon and the sun had to one another at the time of the person's birth is repeating itself. Now, he or she will be confronted with the themes of life. The person will be exposed to the forces of illusion, of deceit, and of wandering paths; it is thus his or her task to discover the true individual path and to make once again the decision for life in one's own terms.

Companion

Master

Here are some questions for attuning yourself: How does or did this second stage of life pass? What forces have developed? How did one deal with them then? How is one dealing with them now? Which space does one have to leave behind, and which space has opened up? What other people have influence upon it? What have they affected? Is/was this stage of life harmonious, or were there setbacks and indecision? What did one have to leave behind? Which specifics make up this stage of life? Attune yourself with these questions to this particular time.

Joker

Card Divination Pattern

General (Foundation)

1. Central theme of the stage ages 15 to 21
2. How do I see myself?

3. How do others see me?
4. What is benevolent for me right now?
5. What gives me courage?
6. What is the danger?
7. How can I put an end to it?
8. What do I leave behind?
9. What do I take with me?
10. What do I need to foster/to observe?
11. What new things are developing?

Base (*Elemental power*)

12. Which natural force needs to be observed?

Companion (*Support*)

13. Which force is accompanying this time?
14. Which force supports in difficult situations?

Master (*Apprenticeship*)

15. Under which star does this time stand?

Joker (*Surprise*)

16. What is helping and supporting me, and healing this stage at this time?

Tip/Advice

With disturbances, you may want to work here with the Special Questions about Individual Sections card divination pattern [see p. 174]. If you wish to explore this theme more deeply, you can continue working with the Destiny of Life [see p. 186], Crisis [see p. 130], The Inner Woman [see p. 74], The Ideal Partner [see p. 48], The Great Fork [see p. 38], Exerting Influence on Unfavorable Developments [see p. 194] card divination patterns and the picture cards in the Hermetic Principles chapter [see pp. 256–269].

22 to 28 Years of Age
Coming of Age and Young Adulthood

General

Object of This Card Divination

With this card divination pattern you can, at any time, examine this particular phase of your life or the time of a person who is currently at this stage of life.

Getting into the Right Mood

> "*The soul must never want to fall, yet shall it gain its wisdom from the fall.*"
>
> (*Johann Wolfgang von Goethe*)

Base

The fourth seven-year stage is a decision-making time. It is the period in which we finally arrive in life. We go on our wanderings and on our journeys to gain experience and learn our tasks in life. Now, we will have to learn to endure and to accept ourselves, to deal with ourselves in order to give something to others later on. For how can we endure and accept others if we cannot do the same with ourselves? We must be able to create a spiritual space into which the "Other" can enter at any time. Thus this stage is all about making us strong enough to face our life's tasks: to be able to go through the usual ups and downs, to live through proper experiences and to open up to the professional world, to our calling and to a relationship. Possibly we may even wish to settle and raise a family. In any case, we must begin to stabilize our own force within us.

Companion

Here are some questions for attuning yourself: How does/did this fourth stage of life pass? What is/was our professional desire, our professional aim? What can be/has been realized of it? Can you endure your own being? How do you regard yourself? What is the picture that you have of yourself? Which abilities are inside of you? Which experiences have you made/are you making as you dwell upon these questions? Does/did harmony prevail? Or were there setbacks and indecision? What have you learned from them and consequently developed inside of you? Which specifics constitute this stage of life? Choose your cards and then begin laying them out.

Master

Card Divination Pattern

General (Foundation)

    1. What is the central theme of this stage of life?

    2. What is my base?

    3. How do I see myself?

    4. How do others see me?

    5. Which force strengthens/weakens my decisions?

    6. On what do I have to work?

    7. What helps me/what hinders me?

    8. What is developing anew?

Base (Elemental power)

    9. Which natural force needs to be observed?

Joker

Companion (Support)

10. Which force accompanies this time?
11. Which force stands by my/our side in difficult situations?

Master (Apprenticeship)

12. Under which star does/did this time stand?

Joker (Surprise)

13. What is helping and supporting me, and healing this stage right now?

Tip/Advice

With disturbances or deviating courses, you may want to work here with the Special Questions about Individual Sections card divination pattern [see p. 174]. If you wish to gain further insight into the themes of this time, you may employ the Ideal and Reality [see p. 132] or Blind Spot [see p. 134] card divination patterns or the picture cards in the Relationship and Partnership [see p. 46–79] as well as Profession and Finances [see p. 80–93] chapters.

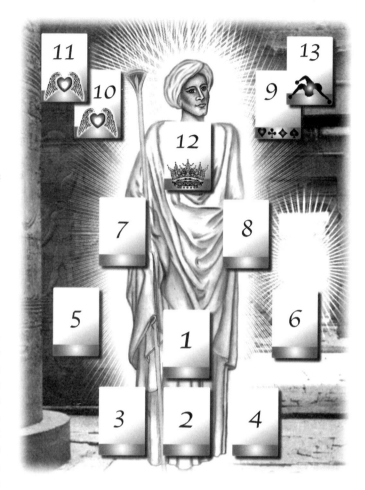

29 to 35 Years of Age

Adulthood: Career, Family

General

Object of This Card Divination

With this card divination pattern you can, at any time, examine this particular phase of your life or the time of a person who is currently at this stage of life.

Getting into the Right Mood

Base

> *"What is the secret of life? A human being proceeds through an inner gate*
> *at which point his or her inner light emerges."*

The fifth seven-year stage is a time of inner review, of one's first reflection. The charm of one's youth is over. We realize that life is entirely different from what we had imagined and had once dreamt of: marriage, career, life itself! We no longer have that much time for ourselves and for the significant others; obligations, rhythms, and tasks started all demand our attention again and again. The realistic, material world exercises its rights and casts a spell over a person. However, we have achieved some of the things that we had been working for. We have created a certain base for ourselves. Opinions and ideas have settled within us. We have a job, we have established a partnership for life, and we have our own family, circle of friends, or even a circle of colleagues. Now it is a time of examination and challenge to continue despite these demands and to complete what we have started. We must continue to ascend the ladder of life into a higher state of being.

Companion

Here are some questions for attuning yourself: How does/did this fifth stage of life pass? What have you achieved so far? What is your goal? What have you started, and what would you like to continue doing? What would you like to change? In what areas do you particularly need staying power? Where are those gaps in which you can encounter yourself once again? What are you experiencing right now or what have you experienced? Is/was this stage of life harmonious? Or were there setbacks and indecision? What have you learned from them/developed in you? What is so special about this stage of life? Choose your cards, and begin laying them out.

Master

Card Divination Patterns

General (Foundation)

1. What is the central theme of this stage of life?
2. What is my base? What have I achieved so far?
3. What is supporting me to go on?
4. What gives me strength?
5. What takes away my strength?
6. What needs to be fostered/observed?
7. For what do I still have to assume more responsibility?
8. What is the change potential for growth for this stage?

Joker

Base *(Elemental power)*

    9. Which natural force needs to be observed?

Companion *(Support)*

    10. Which force accompanies this time?

    11. Which force helps me in difficult situations?

Master *(Apprenticeship)*

    12. Under which star does this time stand?

Joker *(Surprise)*

    13. What is helping and supporting me, and healing this stage right now?

Tip/Advice

With disturbances or deviating courses, you may work here with the Special Questions about Individual Stages card divination pattern [see p. 174]. In order to illuminate special themes of this stage more thoroughly, you may work with the card divination patterns in the Profession and Finances [see pp. 80–93] and Relationship and Partnership [see pp. 46–79] chapters or with the picture cards Crisis [see p. 130] or Destiny of Life [see p. 186].

36 to 42 Years of Age
Strength and Wealth

General

Object of This Card Divination
With this card divination pattern you can, at any time, examine this particular phase of your life or the time of a person who is currently at this stage of life.

Getting into the Right Mood

Base

"He who never stops learning from life is well-advised." (Johann Wolfgang von Goethe)

The sixth seven-year stage is a time of dedication and a time of reception. If we pass the rigorous tests in this stage of life, then we can truly experience the sixth seven-year period as a time of harmony, inner strength, and fulfillment. We have collected many experiences both in our professional as well as in our private lives upon which we can fall back now. We even feel a certain security within us; there are fewer disruptions; we are "undeceived" because we have learned to recognize the deception. We know what we are able to do and what we have achieved. We are experienced in crisis situations and have become able to love. We can now truly love; that is, we can give without expecting anything in return. We can now recognize and accept the gifts of others and thus take joy in them without expecting anything more. We go our way and shoulder the responsibilities that our path brings with it. We stand firm and share our strength with others.

Companion

Here are some questions for attuning yourself: How does/did this sixth stage of life pass? What have you learned? What has changed within you? Is/was this stage of life harmonious? Or were there setbacks or indecision? What have you learned from it, or what has developed within you? What is so special about this stage of life? Choose your cards, and begin laying them out.

Card Divination Pattern

Master

General (Foundation)
1. What is the central theme of this stage?
2. What is my base during this time?
3. What has life given to me?
4. What has life taken from me?
5. What gives me strength?
6. What takes strength away from me?
7. What needs to be fostered/observed?
8. What can I pass on to others now?

Joker

Base (Elemental power)
9. Which natural force needs to be particularly observed?

Companion (Support)
10. Which force accompanies this time?
11. Which force stands by my side in times of emergency?

Master (*Apprenticeship*)

    12. Under which star does/did this time stand?

Joker (*Surprise*)

    13. What is helping and supporting me at this stage right now?

Tip/Advice

With disturbances or deviating courses, you may work here with the Special Questions about Individual Stages card divination pattern [see p. 174]. In order to observe special themes more thoroughly, you can employ the spreads in the Profession and Finances [see pp. 80–93] and Relationship and Partnership [see pp. 46–79] chapters.

General

43 to 49 Years of Age
The Turning Point

Object of This Card Divination
With this card divination pattern you can, at any time, examine this particular phase of your life or the time of a person who is currently at this stage of life.

Getting into the Right Mood

Base

"If the student is ready, the master will appear."
(Eastern wisdom)

This is a true turning point in life. One has passed the zenith of life. In women, menopause starts. We begin to draw our energies within us once more and then expand toward the inside. We are now able to look after ourselves once more, and rediscover our own path. An old spiritual rule states that a man should not appear in public as a spiritual teacher before he is 42 years of age. Once this comes to be, this means that we have now become mature by going through the school of life, and that we have become pillars of support and advisers to others. We turn from being a student to being a teacher. Many of us are astonished by the experience of younger people coming and asking for advice. This turning point is very profound and is often connected with inner struggles, resistance, anxieties, and the feeling of being at somebody else's mercy. Though unnoticed, a new force has developed during this time. Our judgment is no longer as harsh as before, and we are not constantly planning the future but rather beginning to listen silently to the words of others. We also perceive that which truly lies hidden behind the words of sorrow, hardships, and feelings, and so are able to give what the other person needs.

Companion

Here are some questions for attuning yourself: What forces regarding me are unfolding right now? What stands as the Beautiful? What have I already developed within me? What can I give to others? What do I wish to do for myself now? What is of interest to me? What can I tackle now? With what do I feel comfortable? What do I need to pay attention to now so that I can conserve my strength and protect it? What can I carry, or what do I not want to carry any longer? Choose your cards, and begin laying them out.

Master

Card Divination Pattern
General (Foundation)

1. What is the central theme of this time?
2. What is my base?
3. What task has been fulfilled?
4. What have I not fulfilled yet?
5. What has matured?
6. What can I give to others now?
7. To what do I need to pay attention?
8. What is the chance of this stage?

Joker

Base (Elemental power)

9. Which natural force needs to be observed?

10. Which natural force did I master?

Companion (Support)

11. Which force is accompanying me during this stage?

12. Which force stands by my side in difficult times?

13. Which force has developed or is currently developing within me?

Master (Apprenticeship)

14. Under which star does this time stand?

15. What is guiding me with my teachings?

Joker (Surprise)

16. What is helping and supporting me and is healing this stage right now?

17. What can I give to others now?

Tip/Advice

With disturbances or deviating courses, you may work here with the Special Questions about Individual Stages card divination pattern [see p. 74]. In order to illuminate special themes of this time more thoroughly, you can work with The Path through the Middle World [see p. 142], Inner and Outer Stages of Change [see p. 136] card divination patterns, and those described in the Hermetic Principles chapter [see pp. 256–269].

50 to 56 Years of Age
The New Point of View; a Different Perspective

General

Object of This Card Divination

With this card divination pattern you can, at any time, examine this particular phase of your life or the time of a person who is currently at this stage of life.

Getting into the Right Mood

"Seeing we will recognize, in silence we will name."

Base

In the vernacular, this eighth seven-year stage is often called "going through one's second childhood." The children are out of the house, and the era of having to go to work slowly comes to an end. If the individual is running his/her own business, the leadership role is slowly handed over. One can feel age creeping up, but this sense is quickly dismissed from mind. In subconscious response, we call back the juices of youth by any possible means. During this time, it often happens that our partners enter relationships with significantly younger people in order to feel the power of youth through them. We indulge in rejuvenation cures of all kinds and allow ourselves to follow our wishes. It can also happen that we mourn our lost youth and, by doing so, completely abandon ourselves to age, to the past, and to illness.

Companion

Within us, a very strange process begins to take place: While the body ages, the soul begins to rejuvenate. We experience a new kind of openness, tranquility, and astonishment with life, yet we also feel a new form of loneliness. For it makes one lonely to see things that others do not or cannot see yet. And it makes one even more lonely to see loved ones run into misfortune and to nevertheless have to let it happen. Bit by bit, grandparents and the generation of our parents make space for other generations, and thus we move up. However, once again, one's inner light approaches the spiritual world from whence it once existed.

Here are some questions for attuning yourself: How do you experience this stage? What would you like to do with the rest of your life? What have you always wanted to do?

Master

How do you feel about looking ahead? If you are suffering from a disease what does it want to tell you? What is your relation to the spiritual worlds? Can you open up to higher forces? What is your picture of God? How about your religion, your connection back to the spiritual world? Choose your cards and then begin laying them out.

Card Divination Patterns

General (Foundation)

Joker

1. Central theme in this stage?
2. My base
3. What has been completed?
4. What can still be experienced?
5. What does this time give?
6. What does this time take?
7. What is my personal picture of God?

8. What is the chance of development of this time?

Base *(Elemental power)*

9. Which natural force needs to be observed in particular?

Companion *(Support)*

10. Which force is accompanying this time?

11. Which force stands by my side in difficult situations?

12. Which force have I developed within me?

Master *(Apprenticeship)*

13. Under which star does this time stand?

14. What acts through me in this world?

Joker *(Surprise)*

15. What is helping and supporting me, and is healing me right now?

Tip/Advice

With disturbances or deviating courses, you may work here with the Special Questions about Individual Stages card divination pattern [see p. 174]. If you wish to examine certain themes in greater detail, then the card divination patterns in the chapters regarding health and especially in Self-knowledge and Healing [see pp. 128–147] will help.

General

57 to 63 Years of Age

Retrospect and Work on One's Biography

Object of This Card Divination

With this card divination pattern you can, at any time, examine this particular phase of your life or the time of a person who is currently at this stage of life.

Getting into the Right Mood

"He who does not die before he dies, will perish when he dies." (Novalis)

Base

♥♣♦♠

At 56 years of age, we are going through the third moon knot (repetition of the position the sun and moon had in relation to one another at the time of one's birth). In this way, we experience the themes that have run like a central thread through our lives from another point of view. We receive another chance to recognize again a bit more of those themes, to solve them, and to change them. There is great danger that we give in to temptation and abandon ourselves to age, depression, and resignation. We firmly believe that we know the world, and so think that it can no longer offer us anything; everything seems to repeat itself. Life seems to have become a routine, and all progress seems to lie behind us.

Companion

When aging begins to become an issue, just about everyone suffers from some kind of disease thought to be a deadly illness. However, it should be understood that this condition is rather of a psychological nature. It warns us that we as people of this earth carry death within us. Everything that once gave us something on the outside, now only give us little. Our self-image changes; defaults, missed opportunities, and an escape from our own self: All these thoughts step into the foreground of our minds instead of what was once thought beautiful. During this time, we must go alone through this death zone, face the shadow within us, and struggle with our own self. This is a time of deep inner reflection and incessant thinking. All the superfluous and obsolete things are now put down. We reappraise our previous arrangement of life. Everything is newly arranged. We have the great opportunity

Master

to revive new impulses and to bring new realizations forged from proper thinking into the world; through reflection, we can implement those impulses and enrich others with this priceless treasure.

Here are some questions for attuning yourself: What have I done well? What did I succeed in? What did I miss? What do I mourn for? Which realizations do I draw from the path I have been taking so far? What can I pass along? What can I convey to others? Choose your cards and begin laying them out.

Card Divination Pattern

Joker

General (Foundation)

1. What is the central theme during this time?
2. What is my base
3. Which shadow did I not wish to see up to this point?
4. What runs like a central thread through my life?

5. What has fallen in my lap?
6. What have I kicked while it was down?
7. What is the gain in my life?
8. What is the loss in my life?
9. What realizations have I gained?
10. What needs to be arranged now?
11. What is the chance of growth of this stage?

Base (Elemental power)

12. Which natural force do I need to observe?
13. Which force helps me in my retrospect or with my biographical work?

Companion (Support)

14. Which force is accompanying during this period?
15. Which force helps me in the encounter with myself?
16. Which force acts through me?

Master (Apprenticeship)

17. Under which star does this stage stand?
18. What is acting through me now?

Joker (Surprise)

19. What is helping and supporting me, and is healing this stage now?
20. What helps me in difficult times?

Tip/Advice

With disturbances or deviating courses, you may work here with the Special Questions about Individual Stages card divination pattern [see p. 174]. If you wish to deepen your insight into this stage of life, you can employ The Descent into the Underworld [see p. 140] and Visiting the Karmic Council [see p. 286] card divination patterns.

General

64 to 70 Years of Age

Mercy

Object of This Card Divination

With this card divination pattern you can, at any time, examine this particular phase of your life or the time of a person who is currently at this stage of life.

Getting into the Right Mood

Base

"Letting go, showing trust, awakening."

The tenth seven-year stage is a time of mercy, a turn toward the inside. No longer can we deceive ourselves in terms of our age. Illnesses as a consequence of previous, unhealthy styles of living, genetic predisposition, or karmic sufferings rooted in the body from early childhood and youth are now rising to the surface. The soul suffers heavy losses, for close friends and dear relatives—especially people from one's own generation—are passing away before our eyes. Many of the things for which we have fought so vigorously collapse, and we must let go of that for which we have stood up with all our heart. We have to hand over the reins and understand that our successors have their own ways of handling things. The world now distances itself from us. When we are alone, we yearn for company; when we

Companion

are together with people, we yearn for solitude. We are now once more approaching the spiritual worlds. Our picture of faith becomes newly realized. We may open up to higher experiences of God, become a tool of the spirit, and receive new realizations and wisdom that we can in turn give to the world. Or we may circle forever around the old things that do not let us go because we do not let them go: We become lost in them. Many wise men and women received their apprenticeship at this stately age, resigned, and then passed on their insights. A new inner width and a new horizon open up.

Here are some questions for attuning yourself: What realizations come to me? What is working within me? What do I still have to process and digest? What would I like to for-

Master

give and forget? Where am I at peace with myself and the world? What insights is my experience giving me now? What do I let go of? What do I hand down? Choose your cards and begin laying them out.

Card Divination Pattern

General (Foundation)

    1. What is the central theme during this time?

    2. What is my base?

    3. What is now handed down?

Joker

    4. What can I not pass on yet?

    5. What can I easily hand down?

    6. What am I lacking in order to let go?

    7. What is still to forgive and to forget?

    8. What is my picture of faith?

9. What is the chance of growth of this time?

Base *(Elemental power)*

10. Which natural force do I need to particularly observe?

11. Which natural force helps me in this process of freeing myself?

Companion *(Support)*

12. Which force is accompanying through this stage?

13. Which force acts through me?

Master *(Apprenticeship)*

14. Under which star does this period stand?

15. What acts through me?

Joker *(Surprise)*

16. What is helping and supporting me, and is healing this stage now?

17. What is helping me in my development?

Tip/Advice

With disturbances or deviating courses, you may work here with the Special Questions about Individual Stages card divination pattern [see p. 174]. If you wish to examine certain themes in greater detail, then the patterns in the chapter for health and especially Self-knowledge and Healing [see pp. 128–147] will help you.

71 to 77 Years of Age

The Time of Blessing

General

Object of This Card Divination

With this card divination pattern you can, at any time, examine this particular phase of your life or the time of a person who is currently at this stage of life.

Getting into the Right Mood

> *"People who have learned how to pray during childhood, can bestow blessings at old age."*
>
> *(German saying)*

Base

When people reach the age of 70, they enter the phase of a rewarded lifetime. We no longer need words now because our presence alone can bless things and can act as a kind of mercy in a room. Our light shines beyond our being. If we have used our time wisely and have grown from within and if we have not given up on ourselves, then we are working by means of the benefits of earlier deeds—perhaps even from earlier lives—and by extension through an appreciation for the future awaiting us. We have the opportunity for far-reaching realizations. Even if others think that we are absent, we are nevertheless present and notice everything that is going on. We are now working on deep levels of the soul and in deep levels of our being.

Companion

If we reach this high age, then we are blessed. The light radiates from within us even if we are in need of care and are dependent once more upon others. We now have access to stages beyond the limits of time. We see and often experience people that have departed from us a long time ago. We have mystic experiences and learn how truly thin the veil is between the worlds. Often the light of Christ is born in people who have matured and accepted their path of life with all its sundry experiences. One's inner vision has opened and widened. Everything that comes is good, and everything that goes is good; everything is simply taken as it is. The voice of silence reveals itself.

Master

Here are some questions for attuning yourself: How does this stage of life pass? What happens in the face of death? What still needs to be said? What still needs to be taken care of? What should be put into words? Which inner picture must still be altered? What should be left in silence? What should bring peace? Choose your cards, and then begin laying them out.

Card Divination Pattern

General (Foundation)

Joker

1. What is the central theme during this time?
2. What still needs to be said?
3. What should yet be forgiven?
4. What can I pass on?
5. What can be done/left alone?
6. The picture of God/the spiritual realm
7. The inner light

8. What is the chance of growth during this stage?

Base (*Elemental power*)

9. Which natural force do I need to observe?

10. With which natural force am I connected at this point?

Companion (*Support*)

11. Which force accompanies this stage?

12. Which force is now acting through me in the world?

Master (*Apprenticeship*)

13. Under which star does this period stand?

14. Which force acts through me in this world?

Joker (*Surprise*)

15. What is helping and supporting me, and healing this stage right now?

16. What can I pass on in a healing fashion?

Tip/Advice

With disturbances or deviating courses, you may work here with the Special Questions about Individual Stages card divination pattern [see p. 174]. If you wish to examine certain themes in greater detail, you can employ the spreads in the Hermetic Principles chapter [see pp. 256–269] or the picture cards The Ascent into the Upper World [see p. 144] and Personal Light [see p. 216].

From Age 78 On
Completion of the Cycle of Life

Object of This Card Divination

With this card divination pattern you can, at any time, examine this particular phase of your life or the time of a person who is currently at this stage of life.

Getting into the Right Mood

> *"I know that I know nothing, and therefore I know slightly more than someone who*
> *believes he knows and does not know that he knows nothing." (Socrates)*

In this stage of life, the human being becomes a knowing "unknower." When we are more than 78 years old, we enter a time of peace and wisdom. This time is a gift. Words and gestures have become superfluous. The body is slowly giving up its strengths. It is tired. It falls apart. We look into the face of death, and, in this perspective, everything becomes small and unimportant. Earthly matters are no longer of great importance. One's vision is now directed toward the other world. The light of the other side reflects itself within the gaze of the eyes. Depending on how we have lived our life, we will truly experience ourselves in this stage. It is a mystical time when we even more often enter into the cosmic light. Every now and then, we still wrestle with the forces of life and death, with the imagination and pictures of our faith from our time lived, and with old memories; however, by and large, our battles have been fought. We distance ourselves from earth, for the forces of tomorrow belong to another generation. We do not feel so much the outer phenomena of others as the inner reality of the beings around us. We feel the energy that spreads when people enter a room. This time stands under the auspices of wordless understanding. Anything that still needs to be said is now heard with one's inner ear. We are confronted with the knowledge that in the near future we will be crossing the threshold to the other world. With respect to this, we can rethink our life and realign it. This can be a very beneficial experience.

Here are some questions for attuning yourself: How does this stage of life pass? What happens in the face of death? What do I still wish to say? What do I still wish to take care of? What would I like to put in words? What inner picture do I still wish to alter? What should remain in silence? What needs to find peace? Choose your cards and then begin laying them out.

Card Divination Pattern

General (Foundation)

1. What is the central theme during this time?
2. What needs to still be said?
3. What needs yet to be forgiven?
4. What exists in peace?
5. My personal picture of God
6. The inner light

7. What are the prospects of this stage?

Base *(Elemental power)*

8. Which natural force do I need to observe?
9. Which element works within me?

Companion *(Support)*

10. Which force accompanies this time
11. What help can I give to others?

Master *(Apprenticeship)*

12. Under which star does this time stand?
13. What do I give into the world?

Joker *(Surprise)*

14. What is helping and supporting me, and is healing this stage right now?

Tip/Advice

With disturbances or deviating courses, you may work here with the Special Questions about Individual Stages card divination pattern [see p. 174]. If you wish to examine certain themes in greater detail, then the card divination patterns in the Hermetic Principles chapter [see pp. 256–269] as well as the picture cards The Ascent into the Upper World [see p. 144], Personal Light [see p.216], and Transition [see p. 192] will assist you as well.

General

Special Questions
about Individual Stages

Object of This Card Divination

This spread is an additional pattern for the individual stages of life. Here, you can examine and process particulars and specifics that have come up in other card divination patterns more thoroughly.

Base

Getting into the Right Mood

Life does not run in a straight line. As many people as there are, there are also as many paths and courses of life. With some people, there can be special occurrences within the individual stages: separation, addiction, illness, disability, conflicts, crises, etc. There can be many reasons for these happenings, and sometimes it is simply destiny. However, these can always been seen as a request for inner growth.

First of all, attune yourself to the stage where you have noticed peculiarities. Then ask yourself: When did the disturbance begin? What triggered it? What else contributed to how things turned out the way they did? Was it perhaps destiny? What was the specific task of learning and the chance for growth? What was activated through this process? What was destroyed? What needs to be done now since life does not halt merely because of a single event? How can healing be brought about? Choose your cards, and then begin laying them out.

Companion

Card Divination Pattern

General (Foundation)

1. What is the background?
2. Why did it happen the way it did?
3. What did I contribute to it?
4. What has the environment contributed to it?
5. What was the force of fate with it?
6. What has not been taken into consideration with it?
7. What can be learned from it?
8. How can it heal now, and how can it be understood and changed?
9. What is the chance of growth?
10. What is the future path? What do close relations or other people from the outside know?

Master

Base (Elemental power)

11. Which element needs to be observed with it?

Companion (Support)

12. Which force accompanies/accompanied me during this stage?
13. Which force stands by my/our side in difficult times?

Joker

Master (Apprenticeship)

14. Under which star does/did this time stand?

Joker (Surprise)

15. What is helping and supporting me, and is healing this stage now?
16. What helps in difficult situations?

Tip/Advice

If one of the questions seems useless or inappropriate to you, you can easily exclude it or rephrase it in such a way that it becomes suitable for the situation. It is important, though, to take some time for yourself so that the drawn cards can have an effect and unfold the message contained. Especially in situations of misfortune, we have a tendency to quickly eliminate seemingly superfluous things. Yet it is precisely in those things that the healing advice is often hidden. If you still remain unsure, you may continue working with the Clarifying Ambiguous Cards pattern [see p. 44]. The Blind Spot pattern [see p. 134] also often helps to examine the situation more thoroughly.

Life Plan

Object of This Card Divination

This card divination pattern is useful if we wish to come to terms with our life plan and the twelve seven-year stages along which human life develops. The cards of this life plan can be laid out at any time. Earlier stages of life can be observed in reflection, and those that still lie before us show us the tendency for the future under the conditions given. Through this overall view, you will gain an insight into the themes of the stages of life.

Base

Getting into the Right Mood

"Nobody steps twice into the same river." (Heraclitus)

We all are born, exist here for a certain time, and then die. If we attempt to come to terms with the cycle of life and, as a result, the inevitability of death, we can use the time in between more directly and clearly for growth and learning. We all pass through certain cycles and stages on our journey of life. The path of our journey swings, spiral-like, upward, and returns to known points that we then experience through a different perspective. Life has many faces: happiness, joy, farewell, separation, loneliness, birth, death, peace, battle, retreat, appearance, highlights, success, failure. There is a time for everything, and each time has its convoy.

Companion

There are consequences to the great school of life: learn, grow, experience, and mature within the lifetime given to you. We all pass through certain stages and each of us has themes that reoccur over and over again. Great changes usually run in seven-year cycles. The secret to how we experience them, sustain them, and pass through them lies with each one of us; it is determined by our situation in life, our circumstances of life, and our attitude toward life. Each of us has the choice of how to deal with the themes that lie on the way.

Master

In this spread, you can think in an undisturbed manner about your current situation in order to analyze it and see what might be in store for you under the given circumstances. Ask yourself: At which point do I stand? How did each of the individual stages pass? What can be learned in the individual stages? What lies in wait for me? What theme runs like a central thread through my life? Which themes do I encounter over and over again? What needs to be worked on? What needs to be redeemed? What do I wish to accomplish in my life? What is my goal? Where has fate pointed the way ahead for me? What is up to me? Where have I taken on the responsibility for my life; and where have I not? Choose your cards and then begin laying them out.

Joker

Card Divination Pattern

Draw five cards for each seven-year stage.

General (Foundation)/*Base* (Elemental power)

1. The central theme of this stage
2. What happened during this time within me?

3. What happened during this
time in the outer world?

*Companion (Support)/Master
(Apprenticeship)*
4. This force accompanies and
supports me

Joker (Surprise)
5. The gift of this time

Seven-Year Stages:

Birth: my theme of
life/learning

0–7: toddler age; spring

8–14: school days

15–21: puberty

22–28: coming of age

29–35: adulthood; summer

36–42: independence

43–49: menopause

50–56: middle age; second
spring

57–63: reflection

64–70: beginning of old age

71–77: mercy and blessing

Age 78 on: peace

Death: fulfillment; winter

Master (Apprenticeship)
6. Under this star my life stands

Joker (Surprise)
7. This always helps me

Tip/Advice

If the reading looks dark or unclear in one or in several stages of life, you may examine these stages more thoroughly with the following chapter of card divination patterns.

General

Topic of the Day
The Daily, Weekly, and Monthly Companionship

Object of This Card Divination
This card divination pattern is suitable not only for daily but also for weekly and monthly companionship in order to recognize the signs of special events.

Getting into the Right Mood

Base

> *"Each day, each week, and each month stands under a particular sign.*
> *No day resembles another, even if the same work is performed daily."*

Every morning, you should take five minutes for yourself. Listen inside yourself. What have you taken with you from the night? How did you sleep? What did you dream? What does the day lying ahead of you feel like if you now concentrate on it? What is on the agenda for today? What needs to be done? What should be left alone? In the evening then, you can let the day briefly parade by in front of you. How was the day? What was going on today? What made you happy? What was nice? What was less nice? What themes have occupied you today? Which people did you meet? What were the seeming coincidences and unpredictable events? What do you take from this day with you into the night? It might be

Companion

a good idea if you take brief notes in the morning and in the evening. You will experience that you can learn a lot about the invisible through your studies and through the observations in your life. If you so choose, in addition to daily readings, you may also apply this card divination pattern weekly, monthly, annually, every seven years, on those special occasions and so on.

Card Divination Pattern
General (Foundation)
　　1. What is the topic of the day/week/month?

Master

Companion (Support)
　　2. What accompanies me today/during this week/during this month?
　　3. In difficult situations: What supports me in this situation?
Master (Apprenticeship)
Draw this card for special days/weeks/months, if you have the feeling that you need additional strength.
　　4. Under which star does this day/this week/this month/the special occasion stand?
Joker (Surprise)
Draw these cards for special days/weeks/months, on special occasions when you have

Joker

　　experienced negative forces, pain, and inconsistencies, or even when you are facing exams and other forms of testing, etc.
　　5. What helps me and heals me?
　　6. What protects me in this situation?
　　7. What strengthens me?

Tip/Advice

If you wish, you can draw one base card with the question: Which natural force/which element needs to be observed in particular today/during this week/during this month? In order to give this theme even further depth, you may continue working with other card divination patterns in the Course of Life—Themes of Life chapter [see pp. 178–195]. In addition, you may continue working on your posed question with The Way Out [see p. 40] or with corresponding card divination patterns.

The Small Birthday Draw

General

Object of This Card Divination
With this card divination pattern you can recognize under which star your new year of life stands.

Getting into the Right Mood

Base

Light a candle, and in all available peace and quiet think about the year that lies behind you. What have you achieved? What was nice? What was not that great? What would you like to change? Attune yourself to the current moment. Are you satisfied and happy with the gift of your life? Take some time and listen inside yourself. Ask yourself: What do I wish with all my heart to happen in my new year of life? On one's birthday, as people say, the cosmic forces are very close to the birthday child, and the sight into the upcoming year is slightly opened up. You can now call upon the cosmic forces from within and invite them to join you. Attune yourself to them in your singular way. Hold your hands above your selected card decks in order to direct your energy into the cards and then begin laying out the cards.

Card Divination Pattern

General (Foundation)

Companion

   1. That is me

   2. This is the force working at the moment

Joker (Surprise)

   3. That which accompanies me in the upcoming year and supports me; the quintessence

Companion (Support)

   4. That which stands by my side

   5. That which guides me and charges me

Master (Apprenticeship)

Master

   6. Under this star my light stands in the new year of my life

Tip/Advice
Write down the result of your card reading. Place the notes taken into your diary or some-place safe where you can find them again so that you can look at them a year later. In this way, you can check how the forces have worked and you can sharpen a feeling for the mes-sages of your cards. In this way, you can work time and again with the forces that have revealed themselves in the cards for the year, and, better still, you can call them whenever you need. In this way, they become stronger and can continue to accompany you in a help-

Joker

ful manner. For this card divination pattern, cards and oracles that point the way into the future are particularly suitable; for example, you may use Kipper cards, I Ching, runes. However, you may make use of any other card deck as well. Furthermore, onthe occasion of your birthday, you may also work with the Wheel of the Year [see p. 182] or Twelve Houses [see p. 270] card divination patterns.

In the event that you enter a new seven-year cycle (i.e., if you turn 7, 14, 21, 28, 35, 42, 49, 56, 63, 70, 77, etc.), check the Contents page under the stage that lies ahead of you and work with the appropriate card divination pattern. In this way, you can have a peek at the new cycle and thus recognize the changes that lie ahead of you and the forces acting within it.

Wheel of the Year

General

The Great Birthday Draw

Object of This Card Divination

The Wheel of the Year, or The Great Birthday Draw, is a card divination pattern with which you can gain a perspective of the quality of an upcoming, new one-year cycle. This spread is particularly suitable at the beginning of a new calendar year or of a new year of life. It will show you the themes that you could be facing during the months ahead.

Base

Getting into the Right Mood

Light a candle and take a little time for yourself. Think about how the previous year has been for you (you may wish to take a slip of paper and a pen and take some notes regarding the topic). Ask yourself: How was my general mood? What was great? What was not so great? What have I achieved? What have I not achieved? How were the individual months? What were the highlights in the previous year? After you have let the one-year cycle pass in review, attune yourself to your new year of life, to the new cycle of life that lies ahead of you. What are your wishes? What are your concerns? What is waiting to be done? What are your goals?

Companion

You can work with this card divination pattern from one to four different decks. After making your choice, begin with laying out your cards.

Card Divination Pattern

Draw four cards for each month.

General (Foundation)

The central theme during this month

Base (Elemental power)

The natural force during this month

Master

Companion (Support)

The energy that accompanies me during this month

Master (Apprenticeship) or Joker (Surprise)

Under which star does this month stand? And what is helping me during this month?

In the middle of the circle, place one Companion, one Master, and one Joker card with the question: What is the quintessence of the entire new year?

Tip/Advice

Joker

If you cannot deal with the statement of a card, then the Clarifying Ambiguous Cards pattern [see p. 44] will help you with it. If you wish to learn more about the content of the new one-year cycle, work with the Twelve Houses card divination pattern [see p.270].

Expecting Parents

Object of This Card Divination

This card divination pattern enables expecting parents to prepare themselves for a new stage of life which begins with the birth of a child.

Getting into the Right Mood

"Becoming a parent is easy; being a parent, on the other hand, is difficult," says an old German proverb. Your life will now change completely. You are no longer only a couple, but

you will become a mother and a father. From now on, you are responsible for a new human being who is completely dependent on your love and dedication from the very beginning of his or her life. You are no longer the focus but rather the new life is. However, at the same time, this is also a new time of richness for you, since, together with your child, you will be able to discover the world anew.

Here are some questions for attuning yourself: What is going to change now? What is going to fade into the background at least for a while? What is going to step into the foreground? How can you as parents deal with the situation now? What do both parents have to observe? How is the expecting mother doing? How is the father doing? What is going to change in the relationship. Choose your cards, and then begin laying them out.

Card Divination Pattern

General (Foundation)

1. Central theme: parenthood
2. The expecting mother
3. What needs to be observed now in particular?
4. The father to be
5. What needs to be observed now in particular?
6. The expected child
7. What needs to be observed now in particular?
8. What is changing right now?
9. Anxieties
10. Desires
11. What needs to be done or left alone?
12. What needs to be particularly observed?
13. What is the chance of growth of this time?

Companion (Support)

14. What helps the expecting mother?
15. What helps the father to be?
16. What helps the growing child?
17. Which force accompanies and supports us during this time?
18. Which force is with us in our difficult situations?

Master (Apprenticeship)

19. Under which star does our current development stand?

Joker (Surprise)

20. What helps the expecting mother
21. What helps the father to be?
22. What helps the expected child?
23. What gives us strength?
24. What strengthens us in our difficult situations?

Tip/Advice

In the event of disturbances or deviating courses, you can continue working with the Special Questions about the Individual Stages pattern [see p. 174]. In order to give the theme even deeper meaning, the Conception, Pregnancy, Birth [see p. 148] and Transition [see p. 192] card divination patterns readily offer themselves.

Destiny of Life

General

Object of This Card Divination
This card divination pattern will help you find out more about your destiny in life and your life's task.

Getting into the Right Mood

Base

> *"As rose the sun to the planets' salute, on the day that gave you to the earth, forthwith*
> *you grew and prospered by the law that granted your birth. So must it be—yourself*
> *you cannot flee—thus say sibyls and sages; And neither Time nor Might can what is writ*
> *rip from pages or what develops, lives and ages. (Goethe, 1749-1832)*

Each human being enters life according to a plan; a person has a destination in life, a task to complete. Whether or not this person decides to follow the plan depends on his or her own inner decision. Nevertheless, the themes of life will come up for this person again and again in cycles and will continue to confront him or her with its very existence. Every one of us has certain abilities, inclinations, and goals. Yet we do not seem to be able to evade certain themes, and we find ourselves having to tackle them over and over again. And then there are the ideas that do not let go of us, those that persecute us and push us forward until

Companion

we have no choice but to put them into practice. If we observe those themes and ideas carefully and bring them into connection with our abilities, a pattern and a direction become gradually recognizable: our plan, our destination, and our task.

Here are some questions for attuning yourself: What is your task in life? What have you brought with you? What are your predetermined abilities and characteristics? Which ones have been acquired? What has become rooted within you by means of society, country, and the structures into which you have been born? What do you see as your destination in life? What is the sense of your life? What are your abilities? What have you always liked to do from the peace within your mind? When you've gained access to the theme,

Master

choose your cards and begin laying them out.

Card Divination Pattern
General (Foundation)

1. Central theme: The destination of life
2. Endowments
3. Inclinations
4. Roots/force of the earth
5. Feelings/force of water
6. Reason/force of air
7. Heart/force of ether
8. Will/force of action/force of fire
9. The self, potential

Joker

For 9, you may draw two more cards: What lies within me? What lies outside me?

10. What determines my fortune?
11. The law according to which you entered your journey.
   To point 11: What I need to redeem/process
12. That which lies hidden within me
   To point 12: What I know, and don't know, about myself.

Base (Elemental power)
13. This natural force/this element acts through me
14. This natural force/this element must be brought into balance

Master (Apprenticeship)
15. Under this star my life stands
16. My wisdom of life or the destination of my life

Companion (Support)
17. This force accompanies me
18. This one works through me out into the world

Joker (Surprise)
19. The slumbering potential
20. My healing force

Tip/Advice

With the following card divination patterns of this chapter, you can go even deeper into the subject. Regarding any disturbances or open questions concerning the individual elements (positions 4–8), you may work with the card divination patterns for the respective elements. With unclear cards, you can continue working with the method Clarifying Ambiguous Cards [see p. 44].

General

Early Death

When a Cycle of Life Could Not Be Completed

Object of This Card Divination

With this card divination pattern, another step in the reappraisal of two people's relationship can be taken when one of them unduly departed from life at an early point. During the grieving process, many questions arise concerning the unutterable and inexplicable, and it may be that one of the cards might give information and comfort in this dark time.

Base

Getting into the Right Mood

"Each person mourning is a hero of whom incredibly much is expected: in a completely altered inner-and outer world, he or she must achieve superhuman tasks. The time of mourning is more than staying on foreign grounds—it is a journey into a foreign world, and the grieving person learns that language is far away from the world of experiencing feeling! To become acquainted with this foreign world on the inside and the outside is the process of grief. When the mourning person exposes him- or herself to the dangers of this journey and finds the way through the unknown, he or she returns converted. For the abyss of grief is great, but life is even greater" (translated from Anja Wiese: Um Kinder trauern)

Companion

No sorrow is harder to endure than that created by the loss of a beloved person who has been taken from us too soon—it does not matter if it is a child, a partner, or a friend. Many questions remain unanswered. One's confidence in a divine guiding force is shaken and we feel betrayed by God. Waves of unutterable pain, impotence, speechlessness, and deep grief descend upon us and never seem to abate. Although the beginning is very tempestuous, the distances between the waves become greater. One attempts to come to terms with that which cannot be understood and to grasp that which cannot be grasped. It is important that we do not attempt to avoid grief but rather that we go through it; it is necessary that we engage it, that we open up to it, and that we dare to continue to pose those questions again and again which fix us in such a situation. We need to do that as long as necessary until an answer begins to form quietly.

Master

Ask yourself: Why did it happen? What is the sense? How can I cope with it? What do I still wish to tell the deceased? What do I have to leave behind me for good? What gives me strength? Who supports me? Where do I find help? Where are the spaces in which I can open up? Choose your cards and then begin laying them out.

Card Divination Pattern

General (Foundation)

Joker

1. The deceased
2. I
3. Our connection
4. Why he or she had to go
5. That is the sense

6. What I still wish to say
7. What I need to let go now
8. What remains for me?
9. That which gives me comfort and strength
10. That which I can take with me into the remaining time of my life

Companion (Support)

11. A force that is now standing by my side in this time of grief
12. A force that accompanies the deceased
13. A force that helps me to understand and allows me to slowly let go

Master (Apprenticeship)

14. That is the essence of our union
15. Under this star this period stands

Joker (Surprise)

16. What is helping me now to get on with life?
17. What remains for me as a gift of our union?

For outsiders:

Base	1. What can I do for the mourner?
	2. How can I support him or her?
	3. What should I refrain from doing?
Companion	4. Which aid can I place by his side?
Joker	5. What helps and heals him or her?

Tip/Advice

Let the message of the card take effect and develop. It often happens that we cannot immediately accept the message of the cards because the theme of the draw causes us a great deal of pain. This card divination pattern can be repeated in intervals of varying length, as there are always new aspects, questions, and answers in this process.

Death and Grief

General

Object of This Card Divination

"If a man dies, a spirit is born. If a man is born, a spirit dies." (Novalis)

This card divination pattern helps the bereaved to come to terms with the death of another. By doing so the individual can relive once again a small piece of the time shared and thus be freed from the stasis of grief.

Getting into the Right Mood

Base

"In death we are all equal. Nevertheless, each being dies his own death;
for as he lives, so he dies." (Common expression)

Paradoxically, the certainty of one's death is the greatest factor of uncertainty in life. Many people shun the thought of death, even as it already knocks on their door. In earlier times, death was a holy and serious celebration. The dying person was accompanied by the people closest to him or her. The soul was calmed through the love of these people and so was not alone when leaving the body. The Tibetan Book of the Dead testifies to this old form of accompanying death. Today, we are protected from the sight of death, because it causes us to feel strange, anxious, and insecure.

Companion

Death leaves a gap with the bereaved; it may be more than this: It may be a wound, infinitely great pain, or even relief, especially if the deceased had to suffer a great deal before departing. Too often, we have not yet ended our relationship with the other person; we have left things unspoken and have not experienced our relationship to the fullest extent. There is so much left to be said and, at the same time, nothing at all. It is irretrievably over. Nevertheless, the greatest thing that we can do to honor our beloved is to take up something that he or she has given us and mediated to us; echoing something for which the deceased stood keeps that part of him or her alive in us.

Master

Here are some questions for attuning yourself: What have I not said yet? What still needs to be completed? What do I still wish from the deceased? What am I still missing, what do I need to round off this relationship and finally to let go? What gives me strength? What takes away my courage? What do I need to learn now? Where are the chances for growth and the gift of this encounter? What can be learned in this situation that may remain for the rest of my life? What dreams, wishes, and hopes do I have to let go? Choose your cards, and begin laying them out.

Card Divination Pattern

General (Foundation)

Joker

    1. The deceased
    2. I (the bereaved)
    3. What united us?
    4. What is now gone?
    5. What remains?

6. What needs to go for good?
7. What can I see in the future?
8. What still needs to be clarified/to be settled?
9. What gives me new courage and will benefit me?
10. What is the gift of our union?
11. What is now always with me?

Companion (Support)

12. Which force is protecting and accompanying me now during this period?
13. Which force accompanies the deceased?
14. Which force helps me to let go and to keep going?

Master (Apprenticeship)

15. Under which sign did our union stand?

Joker (Surprise)

16. What remains for me as the gift of our union?

Tip/Advice

Allow the drawn cards to work within you and let the message attempting to get through to you slowly unfold. It is often the case that we cannot immediately accept what the cards tell us because the subject causes us too much pain.

Transition

Object of This Card Divination
This card divination pattern helps us to better understand the transitions between the stages of life and those changes within them. In the course of our life, we will have to let many things die only to allow them to be born once more. This card divination pattern is suitable for any new inner and outer stage.

Getting into the Right Mood

Base

As any flower fades and must all youth
Give way to age, so all stages of life grow;
So too does wisdom bloom and any truth
At its time and will not forever flow.
The heart must be ready at any stage of being
For the new beginning, and be ready to say farewell,
In bravery and without grief, to grant new ways of seeing.
And each beginning holds its very own magic spell
That protects us and helps us in ourselves to dwell.

Companion

We are supposed place by place to wander merrily
And never become attached to any place in flight
The cosmic spirit seeks not us to tie, but free,
It wishes to lift us step by step, to grant sight.
Hardly do we feel at home in a circle of life
And become cozy, there is the danger of stagnation.
Only he who is ready for departure and strife
Can escape the paralyzing, habitual paces.
Even the hour of death may in joyous inflation
Send us on a vibrant way to find new spaces.
Life's call to us will never cease...
So be it, heart, take farewell and find peace!
(Hermann Hesse)

Master

There are many gates and transitions both in life and in life's course itself. In order to better understand the forces acting at these gates and transitions as well as what they trigger within us, attune yourself to the theme with the following questions: Wwhich step am I taking right now? What do I take with me? What do I have to let go? What happens on the threshold? What is the sense or the chance for growth of the new level of life? Choose your cards and then begin laying them.

Joker

Card Divination Pattern

General (*Foundation*)

1. What is the threshold/the step/the gate?
2. What is changing right now?
3. What do I have to let go now?
4. What is brought along from an earlier time?
5. What is the currently dominating force?
6. What fosters/what hinders the process?
7. What is the chance of growth?
8. What does the new step bring about?

Base (*Elemental power*)

9. Which natural force needs to be particularly observed?

Companion (*Support*)

10. Which force accompanies me in the time of transition?
11. Which force helps me in difficult times?

Master (*Apprenticeship*)

12. Under which star does this process stand?

Joker (*Surprise*)

13. What helps me and heals me?

Tip/Advice

The Birth to Age 7 [see p. 150] and Death and Grief [see p. 190] card divination patterns will help you to explore your personal situation even more thoroughly.

Exerting Influence on Unfavorable Developments

General

Object of This Card Divination

This card divination pattern serves to examine, understand, and possibly be able to shape a different direction in unfavorable developments in the course of life of ourselves, children, partners, friends, family members, and anybody close to us.

Base

Getting into the Right Mood

> *"Light and shadow are two sides of one and the same medal."* (*Common wisdom*)

As we go through our life, we encounter many beautiful, elevating things; however, we also encounter many dangers, temptations, distractions, and challenges. Thus, it can happen that we, like the people close to us, drift from the right path in life and wander into a danger zone. Yet, this too can be part of our personal development. Perhaps it is an experience that we want to have or a task we have decided to undertake. We can, however, also become stuck in this sidetrack. We must remember, though, that some dark experiences are predisposed in our personality or that they need to exist at a certain time as they promote growth.

Companion

It is often not that easy to be present and watch as a loved one runs into his or her misfortune, even as we can clearly see it happening. Depending on the circumstances that led to this situation, we can interfere (albeit in a helping fashion) or we can let it happen. We must keep in mind that the will of any person is free. Only when he or she decides to change the situation out of free will can outside help have a fruitful effect. No matter what his or her decision is, we will have to respect it. The only thing we can do is to try to positively influence what happens with our good energy, our love, and our strength.

Here are some questions for attuning yourself: When exactly did I, or the person for whom I am laying out the cards, get into this situation? What were the circumstances that led to it? How far has this situation developed? What can I/the person do? What do I/does the person have to refrain from doing? What is mine/his/her picture? What have I contributed to the fact that it had to come that far/what has the person contributed to it? What positive impact can this experience bring? What are mine/his/her hopes, anxieties, and wishes? What is my/his/her assessment of this situation? Is there an image of another human being that prevents me/him/her from getting back onto the right path? Which pattern is behind it? How can it be changed? Choose your cards, and then begin laying them out.

Master

Card Divination Pattern

General (Foundation)

Joker

1. Central theme: the current situation
2. The secret/the hidden force
3. The root/the cause
4. The influence from the past

5. The influence from the present
6. The power of destiny
7. What needs to be accepted?
8. What can be changed?
9. What precisely needs to be done?
10. Future/the way out

Base (Elemental power)

11. + 12. Which natural forces are to be observed in particular?

Companion (Support)

13. On which force should I concentrate?
14. What helps and supports?
15. Which force has a positive effect on the development?

Master (Apprenticeship)

16. Under which cosmic influence does the development stand?

Joker (Surprise)

17. What is the gift of this development?
18. What heals?
19. What gives new strength?

Tip/Advice

If you wish to analyze this theme even further, you may continue working with the Blind Spot [see p. 134] or Crisis [see p. 130] card divination patterns.

Art of Living

General

Object of This Card Divination

With this card divination pattern you can examine the energy in your domicile more thoroughly.

Getting into the Right Mood

> *"The design of your living space is a mirror of your soul."* (Anonymous)

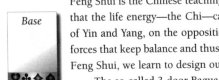

Base

Feng Shui is the Chinese teaching, art, and science of designing living spaces in such a way that the life energy—the Chi—can flow freely. Feng Shui is based on the cosmic principle of Yin and Yang, on the opposition and the harmony of the female and male part, the two forces that keep balance and thus generate ever-new creativity, life energy, and Chi. Through Feng Shui, we learn to design our living spaces in harmony with the cosmos.

The so-called 3-door Bagua is a kind of Feng Shui template whose help we can use in analyzing our living spaces. We can transfer its scheme onto all areas whether it is the city, a property, a house, an apartment, a room, or even a desk. The template consists of nine equal fields: always pairs of three next to one another. The template is aligned through a (main) entrance door positioned so it becomes the usual entrance; thus, the entrance door

Companion

functions like the north on a compass. The eight outer fields are ascribed to the areas of life: knowledge, family, wealth, fame, partnership, children, friends, and career. The middle stands for life energy, the center that contains everything and nothing.

Through the analysis of the Bagua zones and the realizations gained from them, we can influence our situation of life; for example, we can change hindering influences in certain areas of life in a focussed and purposeful manner.

Sketch the ground plan of your apartment. Place the Bagua template on top of the ground plan; by doing so, the side with the zones "knowledge," "career," "friends" should make up the baseline that is drawn from the wall with the entrance door. Ask yourself:

Master

Which Bagua zones are here? Which ones are missing? Which ones are unfavorably burdened or are not in balance? Where are the individual fields of knowledge, family, wealth, partnership, etc.? Which of your areas of life do you find in which Bagua zone? Does this foster or hinder you? What do you feel when you enter the rooms of your apartment? Take some time for yourself. Simply perceive. Occupy yourself with your life and living spaces as the mirror of your soul. Then begin laying out your cards (this card divination pattern is created according to the Bagua template).

Joker

Art of Living

General

Card Divination Pattern

General (Foundation)

1. Career/water/personal path of life/journey/task/new beginning/development
   - 1a. Hindering/fostering influence
   - 1b. What helps to improve the energy of life here?
2. Marriage/earth/partnership/relationship/close relations
   - 2a. Hindering/fostering influence
   - 2b. What helps to improve the energy of life here?

Base

3. Family (one's own family/primeval family/ancestors)/thunder/roots/origin
   - 3a. Hindering/fostering influence
   - 3b. What helps to improve the energy of life here?
4. Wealth/wind/abundance/fortune/blessing/prosperity/inner and outer richness
   - 4a. Hindering/fostering influence
   - 4b. What helps to improve the energy of life here?
5. Energy of life/health/vitality (the Chi) in my rooms
   - 5a. Hindering/fostering influence
   - 5b. What helps to improve the energy of life here?

Companion

6. Friends/heaven/people/cosmic forces (e.g., angel)
   - 6a. Hindering/fostering influence
   - 6b. What helps to improve the energy of life here?
7. Children/lake/projects/creativity (everything you produce and create)
   - 7a. Hindering/fostering influence
   - 7b. What helps to improve the energy of life here?
8. Knowledge/mountain/education/intuition/meditation (everything that grounds you and expands your horizon)
   - 8a. Hindering/fostering influence
   - 8b. What helps to improve the energy of life here?

Master

9. Fame/fire/respect (in public)/degree of familiarity (everything with which you radiate on the outside)
   - 9a. Hindering/fostering influence
   - 9b. What helps to improve the energy of life here?

Base (Elemental power)

10. Which natural force needs to be observed in particular or can inform me about the element that is unbalanced?

Companion (Support)

Joker

11. Which force is currently acting in my living spaces?
12. Which force supports me with the change/which force can I call upon in difficult situations?

Master (*Apprenticeship*)

   13. Under which star does my living situation stand?

Joker (*Surprise*)

   14. Which additional force lies hidden in the room?

   15. Which energy helps to heal and improve the rooms?

Tip/Advice

In regards to the card divination patterns for the respective area, you can examine disturbances in the individual Bagua zones more thoroughly.

Flow of Life

Bagua 1: Career, Path of Life, Travel, Development

General

Object of This Card Divination

With this card divination pattern you can attempt to come to terms with your personal development, your path of life, and your career. In addition, you can apply this spread in order to have a closer look at the Career Bagua area [see the Art of Living card divination pattern, p. 196] in your spaces.

Base

Getting into the Right Mood

"Water reminds us of our journey through life, of the element from which we came."

Assignment to the Career Bagua area: element: water; number: 1; colors: blue, gray, black; form: wave; cardinal point: north; season: winter; time of the day: night; animal: turtle; energy: Yin/female, declining; angel: the Archangel Gabriel. In addition, there are associations with moon, fountain, aquarium, and water formations of any kind (river, current, waterfall).

The flowing of the water will help you to give your life a direction. The path of water has a clear direction. It is considered a symbol of making headway or progress. One's career

Companion

is one example of a stream we follow in the course of our life. We never stop learning. If we have mastered one step, then the next one will follow. The well becomes a creek, the creek a river, the river a current, and the current an ocean. We are on a great journey here in order to experience both ourselves and the world around us, and thus to understand both. We are here to explore the world in its inner and outer dimensions. One of our goals is the mastering of life. When we speak of a career, we speak not only of the professional career but also the path and journey of life, one's personal development that is expanded in each and every direction. The further we develop, the more we can give back out into the world, the greater becomes our strength, and the higher we ascend on the steps.

Master

Here are some questions for attuning yourself: What do you know about your water force, your flowing energy? Are you easily distracted and idle? Do you find yourself giving up quickly? Do you let yourself go, or do you go on despite all failures? Do you know your path? Do you follow it? Are you satisfied with what you are doing? Do you fulfill your task in life? Do you know what you desire? Do you know your path and your goal? Do you feel when the time comes to take the next step, to grow, and to climb another step? Are you within the flow of your life?

Card Divination Pattern

Joker

General (Foundation)

1. Central theme: Your path of life
2. Flowing energy
3. Standing energy
4. Existing predisposition/talent/ability

5. This is helping me to follow my stream of life
6. This needs to be observed on my journey of life
7. This step needs to be climbed now
8. This is the next step

Base (Elemental power)

9. This natural force/this element needs to be particularly observed

Companion (Support)

10. This force helps me to follow my flow of life
11. This force I can call upon in difficult situations

Master (Apprenticeship)

12. This is what the cosmos says about it

Joker (Surprise)

13. This is helping me and healing me now
14. This gets the energy flowing and streaming

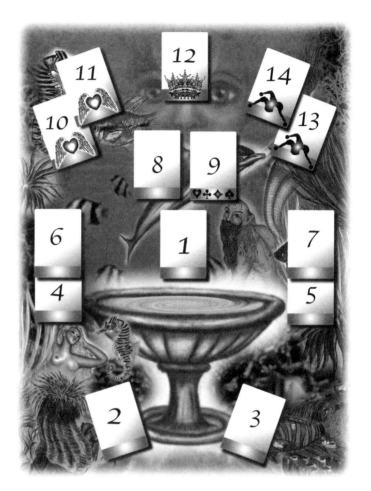

Tip/Advice

For the support and the deepening of the theme, you can work with The Element of Water card divination pattern [see p. 118].

Love Magic of the Earth

Bagua 2: Partnership, Relationships, Marriage, Earth

General

Object of This Card Divination

With the help of this card divination pattern, you can dwell upon the force of the earth in your life. Further, you can employ this card divination pattern in order to examine the Marriage Bagua area [see the Art of Living card divination pattern, p. 196] in your spaces more thoroughly.

Base

Getting into the Right Mood

"The earth is an inviting, receptive, and open element. She arouses the senses with her various forms, sounds, and fragrances and also consequently the desires to share these sensations, to communicate them and to experience them together. (Anonymous)

Assignment to the Marriage/Partnership Bagua area: element: earth; number: 2; colors: pink, orange; cardinal point: southwest; season: transition summer/fall; time of the day: early afternoon; animal: pair of dolphins/ducks; symbol: earth; angel: the Archangel Haniel. In addition, there are associations with plants, illumination, pictures from one's memory, mirror, crystals, and symbols for a happy relationship (e.g., paired figures such as humans, dolphins, ducks).

Companion

Friendships, a social life, partnerships, marriage, and family are forms of interpersonal relationships of sharing, of communicating, and of exchange. They are the bases of community and of tomorrow's generation. Currently, we experience relationship models in a phase of upheaval. Old structures no longer reach out and new ones are just about to come into existence (e.g., the patchwork family: my/your/our children). We are facing a shift toward a society of humanity, of brotherhood (and sisterhood), of equality and community. However, this change takes place slowly. The increased occurrence of singles and the isolation through the media are temporary manifestations of the times and are part of the entire process leading to a new shape. Relationships, partnerships, and a marriage can still endure and grow if both partners find the fulfillment of their needs that have, to a large extent, become manifold. Respect for one another and the maintenance of this respect become of central importance.

Master

Here are some questions for attuning yourself: What idea do you have of a relationship and partnership? Are you happy in your relationship? On which levels are you and your partner (physically, materially, emotionally, spiritually) connected in your relationship? What makes you happy in your relationship? What are you lacking? How is your relationship with yourself? If you are single: Are you leading an active social life? Do you feel integrated within a community or do you feel isolated? Are you having problems entering a relationship? Close your eyes, and concentrate for a few minutes on the topic of relationship. What pictures, feelings, memories come up in you? Afterward begin laying out your cards.

Joker

Card Divination Pattern

General (Foundation)

1. Central theme: Marriage, relationship; partnership
2. The secret of our union
3. The base/origin of our union
4. This is what I contribute to the relationship
5. This is what the union is giving me
6. This is the force of our union
7. This needs to be observed
8. This is the shared task in our union

Base (Elemental power)

9. This natural force/this element needs to be particularly observed

Companion (Support)

10. This force blesses our friendship/relationship/partnership/marriage/family
11. This force is helping us and healing us in difficult situations

Master (Apprenticeship)

12. Under this star does our union stand

Joker (Surprise)

13. The blessing of our union
14. The secret of our union
15. The medicine of our union

Tip/Advice

For help in support and deepening of the topic, you can work with the card pictures in the Hermetic Principles chapter [see pp. 256–269] and other card divination patterns dealing with the topics of partnership and relationship.

Thunder Echo

Bagua 3: Roots, Origin, Family, Ancestors

Object of This Card Divination

With the help of this card divination pattern, you can approach your ancestors. Furthermore, you can employ this card divination pattern in order to examine the Family Bagua area more closely [see the Art of Living card divination pattern, p. 196] in your spaces.

Base

Getting into the Right Mood

"From the land of the ancestors a sound can be heard, elevated into eternity, traveling on through one's blood; the sound of the ancestors, see how it lives in you."

Assignment to the Family Bagua area: element: wood; number: 3; color: green/yellow-green; shape: oval; cardinal point: east; season: spring; time of the day: morning; animal: dragon; symbol: thunder; energy: Yin/female energy, the four cardinal points moving from the inside to the outside; angel: the Archangel Michael. In addition, there are connections with wooden objects, plants, flowers and so on.

Companion

Each human being carries the spiritual, emotional, and genetic makeup of his or her ancestors within. Whoever knows his or her roots will grow wings. Whoever has connections with the origins also knows where the path will lead. The force of these ancestors and family roots can inspire and carry, but it can also hinder and block. When we occupy ourselves with the power of our ancestors and our family, we occupy ourselves with our most fundamental oscillation, with the thunder echoing from the depths toward us. Thunder stands not only for the power of the ancestors, but also for the power of the blood. The force of Thunder stands for renewal, for the beginning of a new cycle. This cycle begins for us with our birth and continues through our children and comes full circle once again through their children in an eternally renewing manner. Thus, the negative, unredeemed power of

Master

our ancestors can gradually change through us while its positive, delivered force strengthens and carries us. If we do not forgive our relatives incapability, inappropriate behavior, thoughtlessness, or so on, then this pain can take up a lot of room in our soul and thus hinder a positive structuring of our life. Therefore, it is good to occupy oneself with one's roots.

Ask yourself: How is your relationship with your family? Are there still unresolved conflicts brewing within you? How is your relationship with your ancestors? What do you know about peculiarities in your family tree? Could there be things that are passed on from generation to generation? Might there be, for example, things that are not only in one's genetic makeup, but beyond as well, such as behavioral patterns, positions, and destinies?

Joker

To which family member or ancestor do you have a special connection? What connects you with your family? Where in your life do original family traditions manifest themselves? Take a family photo and concentrate on your ancestors. Then begin laying out your cards.

Card Divination Pattern

General (Foundation)

1. Central theme: Ancestors, roots, basic oscillation
2. The power of the ancestors
3. Positive/negative influence
4. Expression in life
5. What of the power of my ancestors is in me?
6. What of it comes from the maternal side?
7. What of it comes from the paternal side?
8. What needs to still be processed, what needs to still be resolved and forgiven?
9. What needs to be done now and what needs to be refrained from?
10. What do I live out and what do I pass on?

Base (Elemental power)

11. Which natural force (which element) do I need to observe in particular?

Companion (Support)

12. Which force guides the female line?
13. Which force guides the male line?
14. Which force is supporting me and is now acting by my side in a helpful manner?
15. Which force helps me to work through unresolved issues handed down through the line of my ancestors?

Master (Apprenticeship)

16. The advice of the cosmos

Joker (Surprise)

17. The medicine of my ancestors of the male line
18. The medicine of my ancestors of the female line
19. The potential/the essence of my ancestors within me
20. What can I pass on?

Tip/Advice

For support and for a deeper understanding of this subject, you can work with the Families: The Primal Family card divination pattern [see p. 66].

Cornucopia

Bagua 4: Inner and Outer Wealth, Blessing, Fortune, and Prosperity

Object of This Card Divination

With the help of this card divination pattern, you can become conscious of the wealth in your life. Furthermore, you can apply this spread in order to take a closer look at the Prosperity Bagua area [see the Art of Living Feng Shui card divination pattern, p. 196] in your spaces.

Getting into the Right Mood

Base

"If the unlimited inner treasure is carried into the outside world, it will reflect in matter. For the house of treasure lies in you; it holds everything that you will ever need."

Assignments to the Prosperity Bagua area: number: 4; color: green; cardinal point: southeast; season: transition spring/summer; time of the day: late morning; animal: frog; symbol: wind; angel: Zadkiel, the Archangel Raphael. There are also associations with plants, life- and food-giving beings, running water, flowing energy, nature picture, wind chimes and fans, mobiles and movable sculptures.

Companion

Prosperity is the art of recognizing the seeds that are carried to you by the wind for what they are: pieces of possibility for adoption, needing nourishment so that they grow and reveal themselves to the world. When speaking of prosperity, we do not only mean financial and material prosperity but also fortune, wealth, plentitude, positive energy, gifts of fate, invitations, lucky coincidences, and good encounters—simply everything that becomes a blessing in your life. We are the creators of our circumstances of life; we generate the favorable as well as the less favorable circumstances in our life. Our everyday life reflects our inner reality.

Master

Ask yourself: Are you satisfied with what you have? Do you feel that you are more often favored by luck or were you rather born unlucky? What abundance are you carrying within you? What are your inner treasures and affluences? Is your income sufficient for you? Can you pay for your living expenses? Do you feel blessed by life, showered with presents? Or do you feel punished by life? Do you feel more lack or more wealth within you? Which convictions regarding riches and fortune (in relation to your own person) do you carry within you? Occupy yourself with the topic, and then begin laying your cards.

Card Divination Pattern

General (Foundation)

Joker

1. Central theme: Prosperity, fortune, plentitude, blessing
2. The secret of wealth
3. The inner treasure
4. The outer treasure
5. This hinders/fosters me in regards to living the wealth
6. This needs to be solved or redeemed
7. This blessing I carry as a predisposition/gift/ability within me

8. This needs to be done so that I may experience prosperity in my life

Base *(Elemental power)*

9. This natural force/this element do I need to observe in particular

Companion *(Support)*

10. This force is blessing me now
11. This force supports me in the experience of my inner and outer wealth
12. This force helps me in difficult situations

Master *(Apprenticeship)*

13. The cosmic council

Joker *(Surprise)*

14. Medicine
15. Inner prosperity
16. The path

Tip/Advice

For support and for a deeper understanding of the topic, you can work with the card divination patterns in the Hermetic Principles chapter [see pp. 256–269].

Tai Chi—Vitality

Bagua 5: Vital Energy, Health, Being Collected/Centered/Focused

Object of This Card Divination

With the help of this card divination pattern, you can attempt to come to terms with the theme of vitality. In addition, you can take a closer look at the Tai Chi Bagua area [see the Art of Living card divination pattern, p. 196] in your spaces.

Getting into the Right Mood

Base

"There where day equals night, mountain equals valley, rich equals poor, top equals bottom . . . is the understanding of power that flows through everything and yet is not. To use the power of nothingness means to follow the force that is with you." (from: Die lichte Kraft der Engel)

Assignment to the Tai Chi Bagua area: element: earth; number: 5; color: yellow, earth colored; shape: square; cardinal point: center; symbol: star; energy: Yin/Yang, male and female energy in alternation and in adjustment; angel: the Archangel Sandalfon, Aloha van Daath. In addition, there are associations with interval, rhythm, adjustment, balance, cosmos, and spiral. The vital energy, the Chi, is the universal energy that flows through everything. Where it is blocked, where it becomes disturbed or cannot flow in an unhindered manner,

Companion

the environment and the people in this environment become sick. The freely flowing current of one's vital energy brings about a healing for everything. In the center of all things, there should be a balance between forces. Nothing should predominate. A balance between the elements, the forces in all living things, creates health and wellness. Pains and illnesses of all kind testify to an imbalance. They reveal to us that the vital energy is disturbed in some manner.

Here are some questions for attuning yourself: Which elements in you and your environment are balanced? Which ones are emphasized too much? Which ones are too weak? How does it look in the center of your strength? Are the cosmic forces able to dance within you?

Master

Are you leading a balanced life (work/exercise—resting, strain—relaxation, inhaling—exhaling, being alone—being with friends)? Are you balanced or unbalanced? What should be further brought into harmony in your life? Are you suffering from an illness? Are you carrying a burden with you? Which areas in your life are not balanced; where is an imbalance? What does your lifestyle look like? With what do you surround yourself? Where is there a lack and where is there abundance of energy in you? Are you following your inner rhythm? Close your eyes for some time and concentrate, directing your thoughts upon your life and to the vitality experienced to this point. Then begin laying out your cards.

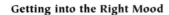

Joker

Card Divination Pattern

General (Foundation)

    1. Central theme: Vitality—the Tai Chi
    2. What fosters or hinders one's vitality?
    3. What fosters or hinders the vitality in my environment?

4. What gives energy?
5. What takes energy?
6. What needs to be observed so that my vitality can be stabilized?
7. What does the current situation want to tell me?
8. What needs to be done?

Base *(Elemental power)*

9. Which natural force (which element) needs to be particularly observed?

Companion *(Support)*

10. Which force accompanies me in my vital energy?
11. Which force can I now call upon in difficult, afflicting situations?
12. Which force activates the vital energy anew?

Master *(Apprenticeship)*

13. Which cosmic force helps to activate the vital energy and to stabilize it?

Joker *(Surprise)*

14. What is supporting the vitality now?
15. What helps and heals the environment?
16. What needs to be done; what does the helpful advice say?

Tip/Advice

For support and for a deeper perspective of the theme, you can work with The Element of Ether [see p. 114] card divination pattern.

Sound of Heaven

Bagua 6: Helpful Friends, Spirits, Angels and Human Beings

General

Object of This Card Divination

With the help of this card divination pattern, you can turn your attention toward the helping forces in your life assisting you from the cosmos. You can also use this spread in order to have a closer look at the Helpful Friends Bagua area [see the Art of Living card divination pattern, p. 196] in your spaces.

Base

Getting into the Right Mood

"If one nurtures within each human being the spirit of God, thus it shines brighter—in the other and in oneself. Whenever the creator gives you something or sends you something, do not hesitate but jump at the opportunity." (Aboriginal wisdom)

Assignment to the Helpful Friends Bagua area: elements: metal, water; number: 6; colors: silver, white, rainbow; cardinal point: northwest; season: transition fall/winter; time of the day: sunset; animal: wise animals (unicorn, Pegasus, owl); symbol: heaven; angel: the Archangel Zadkiel. In addition, there are associations with rainbows, jewels, gemstones, crystals, angels, plants, and cosmic symbols.

Companion

Helpful friends can be those people who have already been accompanying you through life for a very long time. These can be friends but they can also be persons who show up from nowhere to lead and accompany you in an overwhelming situation and then leave you again. It could also be cosmic forces that support you in life: angel, power (or totem) animals, cosmic beings, or master (Jesus Christ, Buddha, Kuthumi). It is the force that strengthens you and gives you authority and energy. If this force is weak in your life, and you know this because you cannot find trust, then an element of expression in your life is missing. Here, it is all about your devotedness, cooperativeness, compassion, and trust. What are you willing to do for others? How do you feel about your ability to do someone a good turn? That which you encounter on the outside is often a mirror of your own inner condition.

Master

Ask yourself: Do you have good friends? What does friendship mean for you? Where do you feel in good hands and accepted? Do you have somebody you think of as a role model? Are you generous? Do you support others? Do you devote part of your time in "service to humanity"? How do you feel carried by life and how do you feel supported by the unseen forces? Do you trust your inner guidance in life? By whom or by what do you feel strengthened? What has always been accompanying you? Who or what stood by your side in the difficult times of your life? Through what do the cosmic forces and helpful friends in your life reveal themselves? Occupy yourself with this theme for some time, and then begin laying out your cards.

Joker

Card Divination Pattern

General (Foundation)

1. Central theme: Helpful friends
2. The support in my life
3. My trust
4. What fosters or hinders the contact with my helpful friends in general?
5. What fosters or hinders the contact with my helpful friends on the outside?
6. What fosters or hinders the contact with my helpful friends on the inside?
7. What do I give to the world?
8. How does it stand with my cooperativeness, my obligingness?
9. What needs to be done or left alone now so that I get into a stronger exchange with the helpful friends?

Base (Elemental power)

10. Which natural force/which element needs to be observed in particular?

Companion (Support)

11. Which supportive force is standing by my side?
12. Which force is now supporting my contact with my helpful friends?

Master (Apprenticeship)

13. Which cosmic force is working now?

Joker (Surprise)

14. What is supporting me now?
15. The helpful council
16. The cosmic tip

Tip/Advice

For support and for a deeper grasp of the theme, you can work with the card divination patterns in the Hermetic Principles chapter [see pp. 256–2690].

Lake of Creativity

Bagua 7: Children, Projects, Creativity

Object of This Card Divination

With the help of this card divination pattern, you can attempt to come to terms with your creative power and your creativity itself. In addition, you can apply this card divination pattern in order to take a closer look at the Children Bagua area [see the Art of Living card divination pattern, p. 196] in your spaces.

Getting into the Right Mood

Base

"There is nothing that you must do; everything is already in you; follow your joy. If you follow the creative power inside of you, you will discover your inner abundance." (Anonymous)

Assignment to the Children Bagua area: element: metal; number: 7; colors: white, pastel tones; shape: circle; cardinal point: west; season: fall; time of the day: early evening; animal: tiger; energy: Yang/male, flowing inwards from the four cardinal points; angel: the Archangel Metatron. In addition, there are associations with metallic objects and crystals.

Companion

Each one of us carries an unmistakably personal reservoir of talent inside that he or she has been given to be creative and inventive, to bring new things into the world, and to express the inner self in an individual manner. This can be experienced through countless means: inventions, projects, impressionist/expressionist art, poetry, painting, music, and dance; however, this can even include one's own children. Projects, inventions, and conceptions are assigned to the same area as children because children are upfront, revealing, joyful, straightforward, honest, and hopeful. They have fantasy and creativity. They express with their entire energy what lies within them, what they perceive, what occupies them, and what touches them deeply in their being. Each one of us carries this childlike expressiveness within. Every human being is able to derive things from within. Think of this mirror of one's energy as the silent surface of a lake. Below the surface lies the depth with all its secrets and its hidden potential that only waits to come to the surface and reveal itself to the world.

Master

Ask yourself: What have you always liked to do best? Where do your abilities lie? What comes easy to you? To what aspect of your inner experience do you have the easiest access? How do you live that which is in you? Are you creative? Do you take time for yourself to live and express what gives you your deepest joy? Are you living in your own paradigm? What have you created from within you? What are your "children"? What do you wish to create from within you? What is hindering you? Occupy yourself with this theme for some time and then begin laying out your cards.

Joker

Card Divination Pattern

General (Foundation)

1. Central theme: Creative power—the children/what you bring into the world
2. What is reflected in my inner lake?
3. What lies hidden in me?

4. What have I brought with me as a predisposition/talent/ability?
5. What fosters or blocks my creative power?
6. How may I access my creativity?
7. How can I put my potential into practice?
8. What needs to be done now?

Base *(Elemental power)*

9. Which natural force/which element needs to be particularly observed?

Companion *(Support)*

10. Which force accompanies me in terms of my creativity?
11. Which force can I call upon in difficult situations?

Master *(Apprenticeship)*

12. What does the cosmos say about this?

Joker *(Surprise)*

13. What is supporting me at this moment?
14. What heals my creative power?
15. What helps me to live to my fullest potential?

Tip/Advice

For support and a deeper perspective of this theme, you can work with The Element of Metal card divination pattern [see p. 126].

Golden Path

Bagua 8: Wisdom, Knowledge/Education, Meditation, Intuition, Realization

General

Object of This Card Divination

With the help of this card divination pattern, you can occupy yourself with the golden path that leads to wisdom. In addition, you can apply the pattern in order to take a closer look at the Knowledge Bagua area [see the Art of Living card divination pattern, p. 196] in your spaces.

Base

Getting into the Right Mood

"It is only with the heart that one can see rightly, for what is essential is invisible to the eye."
(Attributed to Antoine de Saint-Exupéry)

Assignment to the Knowledge Bagua area: elements: water, wood; number: 8; colors: gold, white, violet; cardinal point: northeast; season: transition winter/spring; time of the day: sunrise; animal: owl; symbol: mountain; angel: the Archangel Jophiel. In addition, there are associations with science, inauguration and gemstones.

Companion

The golden path is often used to describe the path of knowledge. We should keep in mind, though, that science and wisdom are far apart from one another. It is knowledge, and the experience of knowledge, that shapes the path to wisdom. The smaller, individual steps are the ones that lead us to the peak of a mountain from where our perspective is so much the greater. We can accumulate this knowledge in various ways: the study of matter, education, mediation, realization, experience, and intuition. In one way or another, we all internalize our realizations and, consequently, knowledge. This is our chance for growth. The more knowledge we gather, the better we come to recognize the connections, and the greater becomes our responsibility for the whole.

The golden path should be a goal of humanity. The mountain is a good symbol for this path. The characteristics of a mountain are silence, peace, stability, immovability. In order to climb a mountain, we need perseverance, strength, knowledge, and, at some points, bravery, trust, and attentiveness: all characteristics of developing wisdom. Furthermore, a mountain is deeply connected with the earth and yet points high toward the sky. It links the earthly and cosmic forces with one another.

Joker

Ask yourself: Are you satisfied with yourself? Do you continue to develop, or do you mark time? Can you retreat from everything in order to meditate, to receive your inner message, and to interpret what you learn? Can you rest in order to collect your strength? How do you put your knowledge into practice in the world? What else would you like to experience? What is your interest? In what areas do you wish to build up further realizations? To where are you drawn? What are your plans for your life? Do you sense an inner silence or peace? Can you receive the messages within you? Occupy yourself for some time with the theme, and then begin laying out your cards.

Master

Card Divination Pattern

General (Foundation)

1. Central theme: Knowledge, growth
2. What blocks/fosters my growth?
   2.a. on the inside
   2.b. on the outside
3. What is connected within me as predisposition, gift, or ability?
4. What is to be done or left alone?
5. What is my current chance for growth?

Base (Elemental power)

6. Which natural force or which element needs to be particularly observed?

Companion (Support)

7. Which force accompanies me?
8. Which force can I call upon in difficult situations?

Master (Apprenticeship)

9. Under which star does my current development stand?

Joker (Surprise)

10. What is supporting me now?
11. The helping council

Tip/Advice

For support and for a deeper understanding of the subject, you can work with The Ascent into the Upper World card divination pattern [see p. 144].

Personal Light

General

Object of This Card Divination

With the help of this card divination pattern, you can attempt to come to terms with your own light. In addition, you can take a closer look at the Fame Bagua area [see the Art of Living Feng Shui card divination pattern, p. 196] in your spaces.

Getting into the Right Mood

Base

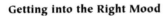

"Light is born on the inside and can radiate from there out into the world."

Assignment to the Fame Bagua area: element: fire; number: 9; color: red; shape: triangle; cardinal point: south; season: summer; time of the day: noon; animal: phoenix; energy: Yang/male ascending; angel: the Archangel Uriel. In addition, there are associations with the all-perceiving eye, the force of change, the melting pot, light, fire, and candles

Fame consists of honor, respect, the extent of fame, but it also contains elements of understanding and clarity. In which combination these connections exist depends on the inner light, that inner fire in each one of us. It also depends on how far it is developed, how far it radiates into the world, and how visible it is. One's own light, one's fire, is the expres-

Companion

sion of one's own force. To develop it within us is one of the paths that we follow in life. It is the nature of light to radiate and shine and thus "put us and others within the true light." It can, however, also "bring to light" grim secrets and dark sides, for our light can sometimes be diminished. To be concerned with fame helps us to recognize the light within us and consequently the shadows as well. If we know them, we can name them and, if necessary, work on them and change them.

Ask yourself: How do you stand with your force of fire and energy? Are you easily distracted or idle? Do you give up quickly, do you let yourself go, or do you go on despite failures? Do you know your inner light? Do you follow it? Do you tend to hide your light under

Master

a bushel? Can others warm themselves from your light? Is your inner light a beacon for others? Do you drag people along or carry them, or do you rather prefer being carried by others? Is it important to you what other people think of you? Does your good reputation have significance for you? Do you let yourself be easily distracted by others? Do you let yourself be easily convinced? Do you prefer to follow the newest trend or do you go your own way? Do you receive the recognition that is due to you and a fair compensation for your achievements? Do you get what you deserve? Occupy yourself with the theme for some time, and then begin laying out your cards.

Joker

Card Divination Pattern

General (Foundation)

1. Central theme: Fame—one's own light
2. What hinders or fosters my own light
3. What shall I leave behind/what is to be dismissed?

4. What is there as a gift/ability in order to strengthen this force within me?
5. How do I see the world?
6. How does the world see me?
7. What needs to be observed or changed?
8. What is helping me to develop my inner light?
9. What is to be done now?

Base (Elemental power)

10. Which natural force/which element needs to be particularly observed?

Companion (Support)

11. Which force helps me to develop my inner light?
12. Which force can I call upon in difficult situations?

Master (Apprenticeship)

13. What does the cosmos say about it?

Joker (Surprise)

14. What is helping and healing me at this moment?
15. What is supporting me now?

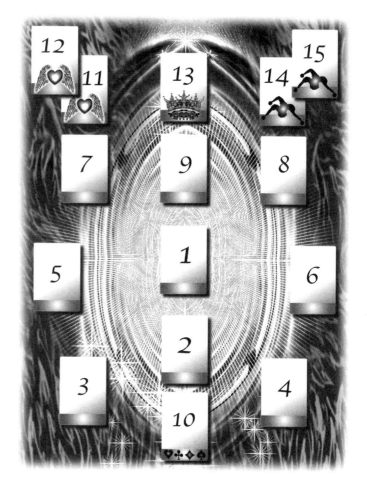

Tip/Advice

For support and for a deeper look at this theme, you can work with The Element of Fire card divination pattern [see p. 122].

Circle of the Year

Forces That Carry You through the Cycle of the Year

General

Base

Companion

Master

Joker

Object of This Card Divination

Here, you can observe which forces accompany you throughout the year. Every six to seven weeks, a new force develops in nature. In the Celtic-Germanic tradition, this is reflected in the sun festivals—Yule, Ostara, Midsummer, and Thanksgiving—that orient themselves according to the course of the sun, as well as the equinoxes—Samhain, Imbolc, Beltane, and Lammas—that are followed through the cycle of the plants and harvest. The sun and earth festivals are alternately celebrated in six- to seven-week intervals. If you can reconnect with this old rhythm, you can use this natural quality of time, marked by the yearly festivities, in planning and observing your everyday life. For there is a time for everything, and we should remember that not every moment is the right one for certain enterprises.

Getting into the Right Mood

The eight festivities in the circle of the year comply with the position of the sun and the cycles of the earth (see the precise assignment with the following card divination patterns). With the following questions, attune yourself to the circle of the year: at what moment in the circle of the year am I currently? What is happening in nature right now? What does this signify for my life? With which forces in nature can I connect now? What is the overall energy for the entire cycle of the year that lies ahead of me?

A diary of the wheel of the year festivities is very helpful for the assignment, for you can take brief notes concerning the force of the respective period of time. You can lay your the Wheel of the Year cards at any time; however, the particularly favorable moments are Samhain (the Celtic New Year), Yule (the winter sun turn), Imbolc (when the days become once again perceptibly longer at the beginning of February), and Ostara (the Spring Equinox). These festivities lie within those dark times of the year dedicated to inner reflection and new beginnings. Each of the three cards drawn applies both to the annual celebration and to the six to seven weeks till the next annual celebration.

Card Divination Pattern

Draw three cards for each festival:

Base:	What is the basic energy form?
General:	What is my task during this time?
Companion:	What protects and accompanies me until the next festival?

1. Samhain/All Saint's Day/Halloween/Earth Festival on November 1
2. Yule/Christmas/Alban Arthuan/Winter Sun Turn/Sun Festival on December 21
3. Imbolc/Groundhog Day/Brighid/Earth Festival on Feruary. 1, 2
4. Ostara/Easter/Alban Eiler/Vernal Equinox/Sun Festival on March 21
5. Beltane/May Day/Walpurga/Walpurgis Night/ Earth Festival on May 1

6. Midsummer Night/Eve of St. John/Alban Heruin/Summer Sun Turn/Sun Festival on June 21

7. Lammas/Loaf Mass/ Lugnasadh//Earth Festival on August 1

8. Thanksgiving/ Alban Elued/Fall Equinox/Sun Festival on September 21

Master (Apprenticeship)

9. Under which star does the entire cycle of the year stand?

Tip/Advice

If you wish to learn more about the respective festivities and in greater detail, you can do so by working with the card divination patterns that follow in this chapter. If

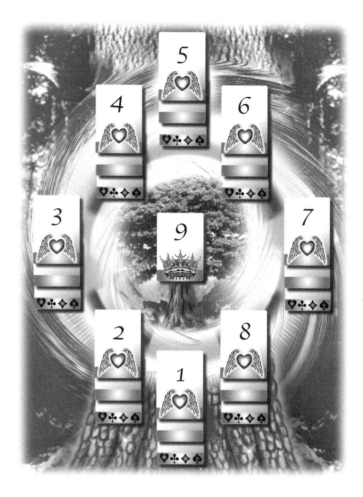

you wish, in addition to the card under Master, you may draw one Joker card by posing the question: Which force supports me overall in this year's cycle?

Samhain

All Saint's Day/Halloween/Earth Festival on November 1

General

Object of This Card Divination

This card divination pattern serves to illuminate the annual Samhain celebration that is observed on November 1 more closely and to get an insight into both the quality and the tasks of the upcoming time. The cards drawn here are valid until December 21.

Getting into the Right Mood

Base

The celebration: Around November 1, people celebrate Samhain, All Soul's Day or Halloween. This festival is dedicated to the earth. In some traditions it lasts for three days in a row, from October 31 to November 2. It is the beginning of the Celtic New Year.

Nature undergoes a series of dramatic changes: It has thrown off everything superfluous. It has withdrawn to its interior and prepares itself for the cold, dark season. The night is victorious over the day. Shade overpowers light. The time of inner reflection and meditation begins.

These are the themes of the celebration: underworld, power struggle, wrestling between the light and the darkness, intensive inner processes, taking leave, letting go, meeting one's shadows. During this time, the veil between the worlds, the realm of the living and the dead, is particularly thin. Thus, Samhain is also a celebration of the dead and of the ancestors, yesterday's forces that still have an effect today. However, angels also act now more intensively and come close to the earth.

Companion

Here are some questions for attuning yourself: Emotionally, what do I wish to take with me into the long and cold winter months? What is superfluous? What, according to Nature's rules, is supposed to die? What is supposed to be reborn? What shadows do I still have to work on? Attune yourself to the time and prepare yourself for the time of inner meditation. You can take some notes to your current situation and then symbolically burn what you wish to let pass away. Choose your cards and then begin laying them out.

Master

Card Divination Pattern

Base (Elemental power)
    1. This natural force accompanies me

General (Foundation)
    2. This was the quintessence of recent times
    3. Central theme: Samhain
    4. The dark shadows of the night; that which is hidden

Joker

    5. The force of my ancestors
    6. This is what I have to attempt to come to terms with
    7. That which is supposed to die; that which I no longer need
    8. That which is supposed to be born anew; that which I should protect

Companion (Support)

9. That which is by my side

10. What strengthens me in dark times and guides me

Master (Apprenticeship)

11. The protective casing for the upcoming time

Joker (Surprise)

12. What gives me strength to get through this time

These are special questions in case a ritual is supposed to take place:

General/Base

13. What needs to be observed with the Samhain ritual?

General/Companion

14. Which force accompanies our ritual?

General/Master or Joker

15. Which force protects our ritual?

Tip/Advice

If you wish to learn more about the shadows, you can work with The Descent into the Underworld card divination pattern [see p. 140].

Yule

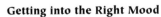

Christmas/Alban Arthuan/Winter Sun Turn/Sun Festival on December 21

General

Object of This Card Divination

This card divination pattern serves to take a closer look at Yule, the day of the rebirth of light that is celebrated on December 21 and to obtain an insight into the quality and the tasks of the upcoming time. The cards drawn here are valid until February 1.

Getting into the Right Mood

Base

The celebration: Yule is celebrated on December 21. It is a celebration full of light, holiness, and joy. It is a celebration of reflection, expectation, and rebirth in which the winter sun turn and a new beginning are celebrated. The Christian correlation is Christmas celebrated on December 24 as the birthday of Jesus. In the Druidic tradition, the celebration is called "Alban Arthuan" which means "the Light of Arthur." Yule night is the longest night of the year in which we celebrate the birth of the Sun Child, echoing the importance of light and its immanent victory over darkness.

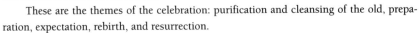

Nature undergoes a series of dramatic changes: Nature has withdrawn into the innermost point of the earth. Often, a blanket of snow covers the ground. The resplendence of far-off worlds is reflected in the snow. Nothing stirs outside, but the angels are particularly

Companion

close to earth in order to accompany the birth of light and to proclaim it. It is a time of joyous expectation and excitement. In the month of December, the darkness devours the light until it is reborn on December 21.

These are the themes of the celebration: purification and cleansing of the old, preparation, expectation, rebirth, and resurrection.

Ask yourself: Into what would you like to be allowed? Of what would you like to cleanse yourself? To what would you like to give birth anew? Which new goals and projects do you have? What would you like to give to the world? What do you desire from the

Master

world? Which new quality and force announces itself for the new year? Attune yourself to the celebration and the upcoming time until Imbolc. You may wish to take some notes. Choose your cards and then begin laying them out.

Card Divination Pattern

Base (Elemental power)
   1. Which natural force accompanies me?
General (Foundation)
   2. What is the quintessence of recent times?

Joker

   3. Central theme: Yule night
   4. What do I leave behind now?
   5. What will be born anew?
   6. Which present do I receive now?
   7. Which present do I give to the world?

222 THE GIANT BOOK OF CARD DIVINATION

Companion (Support)

8.+ 9. Which heavenly forces are standing by my side, are accompanying me, or are working now with me?

Master (Apprenticeship)

10. Under which star does the upcoming time stand?

Joker (Surprise)

11. Which force does the cosmos give to me?

These are special questions in case a ritual is supposed to take place:

General/Base

12. What needs to be observed with the Yule ritual?

General/Companion

13. Which force accompanies our ritual?

General/Master or Joker

14. Which force protects our ritual?

Tip/Advice

This time is particularly favorable for casting oracles. Angelic choirs cry out in jubilation, and natural beings of all kind are overjoyed about the rebirth of light. All this gladness allows human beings to gaze into a mirror of the cycle of the new year during the upcoming twelve night spirits. The Twelve Houses [see p. 270], Three Wishes from the Good Fairy [see p. 238], and Wheel of the Year [see p. 182] card divination patterns can grant an even deeper insight into the upcoming year.

Imbolc

General

Object of This Card Divination

This card divination pattern serves to allow a closer look at the annual Imbolc celebration observed at the beginning of February in order to obtain an insight into both the quality and the tasks of the upcoming time. The cards drawn here are valid until March 21.

Getting into the Right Mood

Base

The celebration: Imbolc is traditionally celebrated on the night from the first to the second of February. The Western equivalent is Groundhog Day. Moreover, it is the celebration of Brighid, the Celtic goddess of light, poetry, and healing. Imbolc means "in the belly." In the belly, new life grows until it is born. The time is shaped by forces that are gentle and full of light; however, this time also has extremely powerful, cleansing, healing, and fiery sides. Now, we have the possibility to cleanse our soul, to form it and to clear it. It is the time when we can make our visions, inspirations, and dreams of the new year visible through the power of our inner fire. As a period of great quiescence and patience, it is a time to emotionally prepare personal plans and to mentally reflect upon ourselves.

Companion

Nature undergoes a series of dramatic changes: February is a month in which the strength of the sun noticeably increases. Although it is most likely still cold outside and somewhat inhospitable, within the womb of Mother Earth, the forces and juices of nature begin to rise again in preparation for their breakthrough. Nature awakens to new life. Spring announces itself with snowdrops and crocuses; now lambs and kids are born.

These are some of the themes of the celebration: inner and outer cleansing and silent personal planning; to anchor the light to the earth; to call upon mental forces so that they reveal themselves in the new year cycle.

Master

Ask yourself: Of what would you like to cleanse yourself? Which force would you like to strengthen and foster in the course of the new year? As with the sun, which force would you like to anchor to the earth? What should reveal itself in the new year? What is important for your soul so that it can heal? Attune yourself to the celebration. The forces act till Ostara, which is celebrated on March 21. Choose your cards and then begin laying them out.

Card Divination Pattern

Base (Elemental power)
1. Which natural force accompanies me?

Joker

General (Foundation)
2. What was the quintessence of recent times?
3. Central theme: Imbolc
4. What do I wish to cleanse?
5. What is helping me to realize my desires, dreams, and visions?

6. What is hindering me?
7. What needs to be strengthened and fostered?
Companion (Support)
8. Which force accompanies and supports me during this time?
Master (Apprenticeship)
9. Under which star does the upcoming time stand?
Joker (Surprise)
10. Which force is helping me and healing me?

These are special questions in case a ritual is supposed to take place:
General/Base
11. What needs to be observed with the Imbolc ritual?
General/Companion
12. Which force accompanies our ritual?
General/Master or Joker
13. Which force protects our ritual?

Tip/Advice

Since now is the time of personal healing and of inner planning, you may continue working with The Grail Cup card divination pattern [see p. 128]. If, however, you wish to explore new paths or if you are facing decisions, The Great Fork card divination pattern [see p. 38] will be helpful. Furthermore, The Path through the Middle World card divination pattern [se p. 142] is a good method to examine currently acting forces more thoroughly.

Ostara

Easter/Alban Eiler/Vernal Equinox/Sun Festival on March 21

General

Base

Companion

Master

Joker

Object of This Card Divination

This card divination pattern serves to take a closer look at the annual Ostara celebration, the Vernal Equinox, in order to obtain an insight into both the quality and the tasks of the upcoming time. The cards drawn here are valid until May 1.

Getting into the Right Mood

The celebration: Ostara is celebrated in the Celtic-Germanic tradition on March 21. The goddess Ostara, the goddess of growth, fertility, and the rising light of dawn, gave this festival its name. It corresponds to the Christian Easter celebration to which the crucifixion and the resurrection of Jesus Christ are ascribed. In the Druidic tradition, this festivity is called "Alban Eiler" which means "Light of the Earth." The light is now victorious over the darkness. It is a joyful festivity full of happiness, lightheartedness, and laughter. The Sun Child, who was born around winter sun turn, has grown up. Still innocent, tempestuous, childlike, it dances and smiles full of a zest for life into the new morning. It is a time of action, desire, and strength.

Nature undergoes a series of dramatic changes: Spring has become visible. Trees blossom and are covered by fresh green. Everything begins to bloom. Nature has shaken off the winter, and everything strains to push through to the outside. Birds are returning and loudly sing their morning and evening songs. The days are now once again longer than the nights. Clocks are set to summertime.

These are some of the themes of the time: The celebration of the childlike, tempestuous zest for life in us; the blessing of the forces of nature so that they grow and thrive; sowing and planting for the later harvest; making the earth fertile so that the light becomes visible and can reveal itself in the shape and form of plants.

Here are some questions for attuning yourself: Which project would you like to bless? Which plans would you like to put into practice at this point? What would you like to learn? In which directions would you like to grow? What needs to be done so that your desires, dreams, and visions are brought to life? What would you like to unfold? What would you like to bring into the world? What needs to be done in concrete terms? Connect with the forces of spring and take action. Choose your cards and then begin laying them out.

Card Divination Pattern

Base (Elemental power)
   1. Which natural force accompanies me?
General (Foundation)
   2. What is the quintessence of recent times?
   3. Central theme: Ostara
   4. What needs to be done now?

5. Which force needs to be strengthened or observed and, in doing so, helps me to achieve my breakthrough?
6. What helps or hinders me to realize my plans/visions or desires?

Companion *(Support)*

7. Which force supports me as I set out to work?

Master *(Apprenticeship)*

8. Under which star does the upcoming time stand?

Joker *(Surprise)*

9. What is supporting me now?

These are special questions in case a ritual is supposed to take place:

General/Base

10. What needs to be observed with the Ostara ritual?

General/Companion

11. Which force accompanies our ritual?
12. Which force supports the ritual leader(s)? (in the event of several, each person gets a card)

General/Master or Joker

13. Which force protects our ritual?

Tip/Advice

If you wish to explore more deeply the themes of this festivity, you may continue working with The Element of Fire card divination pattern [see p. 122].

General

Beltane

May Day/Walpurga/Walpurgis Night/ Earth Festival May 1

Object of This Card Divination

This card divination pattern serves to take a closer look at the annual Beltane celebration, the Celtic-Germanic beginning of summer, and to get an insight into both the quality and the tasks of the upcoming time. The cards drawn here are valid until June 21.

Getting into the Right Mood

Base

The celebration: Beltane means "light" and "fire." The name is derived from the Druidic Sun God Belanos, who was attracted by the fragrances of spring and descended from heaven in order to marry the goddess of the earth. Beltane is celebrated on May 1, which is in the Christian tradition May Day. It is a festivity of the senses, of untamed lust and passion, of fertility, yet also of the deception of the senses. The Sun Child has now grown into the years of his youth that are full of joie de vivre and passion: He has sexually matured. A uniting is about to take place. Therefore, fertility rites of all kind are also celebrated during this time.

Nature undergoes a series of dramatic changes: The merry month of May announces the arrival of summer. Nature has awakened to its full splendor. It exudes its intoxicating aromas in order to encourage fertilization. The lovely fragrance of the trees and flowers that are blossoming—e.g., that of roses and lilac—inflames our senses. Nature sings with the voice of the birds and seduces us with warm sun rays on our bare skin.

Companion

These are some themes of the celebration: Unification, making relationships fertile, and deepening and strengthening bonds. It is a time of strength, love, relationships, and matters of the heart.

Ask yourself: Which relations would I like to deepen, strengthen and foster? What should carry fruits? What would I like to deepen, to guard, and cherish in the near future so that it bears fruits? Occupy yourself with theses themes. Then choose your cards and begin laying them out.

Master

Card Divination Pattern

Base (Elemental power)

    1. Which natural force accompanies me?

General (Foundation)

    2. What is the quintessence of recent times?

    3. Central theme: Beltane

    4. What is helping me to deepen my projects and to enable them to become fertile?

    5. Which force fosters or hinders matters concerning my sense of love?

Joker

    6. Where have I currently succumbed to a deception or an illusion?

    7. What is worth being observed by me now?

Companion (Support)

    8. What is accompanying me during this time?

Master (Apprenticeship)
  9. Under which star does my time stand?
Joker (Surprise)
  10. What is supporting me now?

These are special questions in case a ritual is supposed to take place:

General/Base
  11. What needs to be observed with the Beltane ritual?
General/Companion
  12. Which force accompanies our ritual?
General/Master or Joker
  13. Which force protects our ritual?

Tip/Advice
This is a good opportunity to clarify matters of relationship and the heart. You can further deepen these themes with the Heart Chakra [see p.102], Couple Talk [see p. 60], and Relationship Analysis [see p. 62] card divination patterns.

Midsummer

General

Object of This Card Divination

This card divination pattern serves to take a closer look at the annual midsummer celebration, the summer sun turn, and to get an insight into both the quality and the tasks of the upcoming time. The cards drawn here are valid until August 1.

Getting into the Right Mood

Base

The celebration: Midsummer is celebrated on June 21; this is, according to our calendar the beginning of summer; however, in the Celtic-Germanic circle of the year, it is the middle of the summer, hence, the name. In the Christian tradition, it became the Eve of St. John. In the Druidic tradition, it is a holy festivity of the brotherhood of the suns and is called "Alban Heruin" which means "Light of the Shore." It is the longest day of the year, for afterward the light of the sun wanes once again and the days become shorter. Therefore, the first drop of melancholy resonates in this festivity.

Nature undergoes a series of dramatic changes: Summer is in full blossom. Nature has unfolded its full splendor. It is a time of freedom and independence. Only light summer clothes surround the human body. People spend a lot of time together outside until late into the mild summer nights. Nature beings are particularly close to the people during this time. At this point of time, the sun reaches its greatest strength.

Companion

These are some of the themes of the celebration: Friendship and comradeship; realization, inspiration; balance between forces; foretelling and prophesying; receiving teachings.

Ask yourself: Which force needs to be held on to and permanently stabilized? What have I done up to this point? What needs to be brought to an end now? Where did I reach independence? In which areas did I come into my full force? Where did I allow myself to be deceived? Where did I see clearly? Occupy yourself with the theme. Choose your cards and then begin laying them out.

Master

Card Divination Pattern:

Base (Elemental power)
>   1. Which force in nature is guiding me now?

General (Foundation)
>   2. What is the quintessence of time that lies behind me?
>   3. Central theme: midsummer
>   4. What was I able to deepen?
>   5. What do I have to work on?
>   6. What needs to be observed now so that I can harvest?

Joker

Companion (Support)
>   7. Which force is accompanying me during the upcoming time?

Master (Apprenticeship)
   8. What wisdom is helping me now?
Joker (Surprise)
   9. Which force is guiding me during the upcoming time?

These are special questions in case a ritual is supposed to take place:
General/Base
   10. What needs to be observed with the midsummer ritual?
General/Companion
   11. Which force accompanies our ritual?
General/Master or Joker
   12. Which force protects our ritual?

Tip/Advice

If you wish to explore more deeply the theme of this festivity, you can work with The Star Oracle [see p. 28] and The High Priestess [see p. 32] card divination patterns.

Lammas

Loaf Mass/Lugnasadh//Fall Equinox August 1

General

Object of This Card Divination

This card divination pattern serves to take a closer look at the annual Lammas celebration, the festivity of the first hay harvest, and to get an insight into both the quality and the tasks of the upcoming time. The cards drawn here are valid until September 21.

Getting into the Right Mood

Base

The celebration: The festival on August 1 in the Celtic-Germanic tradition is called Lammas. The Christians made the Loaf Mass out of it. In the Druidic tradition, it is called Lugnasadh and is dedicated to the old Grain God Lugh. It is a sun festival and once marked the beginning of the grain harvest. With the rituals for this festival, besides the first harvest, the herbs are also consecrated so that their healing power is preserved. In earlier times, people got married during this time. Back then, marriage on trial still existed, and when the married partners came to the conclusion that they were not made for each other after all, they could once more separate a year later.

Companion

Nature undergoes a series of dramatic changes: That which had been sown has now reached maturity. Nature has unfolded its full power; it is opulent, and its cornucopia is flowing over. The time of growth has come to an end, and the harvest is imminent. The sun has crossed the zenith point; it is still strong, but it now begins to lose its strength, and fall announces itself. The sun is worshipped in the grain that has now become ripe and yellow.

These are some themes of the celebration: Blessing of the imminent harvest; trusting that one is carried and nurtured; the sharing of joy concerning the future harvest.

Ask yourself: What is contained in my cornucopia? Which matters have proven to be fruitful? What should be celebrated and appreciated? What do I wish to share with others now? Attune yourself to the festivity and the quality of the time. Choose your cards and then begin laying them out.

Master

Card Divination Pattern

Base (Elemental power)
    1. Which natural force accompanies me?
General (Foundation)
    2. What is the quintessence of the time that lies behind me?
    3. Central theme: Lugnasadh
    4. What carries fruits?

Joker

    5. What has not carried fruits?
    6. What am I sharing with others now?
    7. What forces need to be fostered or observed now?
Companion (Support)
    8. Which force accompanies me during the upcoming time?

Master (Apprenticeship)
9. Under which star does the upcoming time stand?

Joker (Surprise)
10. Which force will support and carry me during the time to come?

These are special questions in case a ritual is supposed to take place:

General/Base
11. What needs to be observed with the Lugnasadh ritual?

General/Companion
12. Which force accompanies our ritual?

General/Master or Joker
13. Which force protects our ritual?

Tip/Advice
If you wish to explore even more deeply the themes of this festivity, you can continue working with the Cornucopia [see p. 206] and The Element of Earth [see p. 120] card divination patterns.

General

Thanksgiving
Fall Equinox/Alban Elued/Sun Festival on September 21

Object of This Card Divination
This card divination pattern serves to take a closer look at Thanksgiving, which is celebrated during the fall equinox, in order to get an insight into both the quality and the tasks of the upcoming time. The cards drawn here are valid until November 1.

Getting into the Right Mood

Base

The celebration: In the Christian tradition, the fall equinox is called Thanksgiving, and therefore, we celebrate on this day the same thing as the Celtic and Germanic peoples before us. In the Druidic tradition, this festival is called "Alban Elued," which means "Light of Water." It is the second of the harvest celebrations; whereas Lammas constitutes the beginning, Thanksgiving signals the ending of the harvest time. Even today, most parish fair festivities are during this time. Day and night are equally long; subsequently, darkness slowly begins to take power.

Companion

Nature undergoes a series of dramatic changes: The harvest has been brought in; we are beginning to say farewell to summer; the sun loses its strength, and fall takes over the reins. Nature begins to shed everything that is superfluous. The plants begin their preparation for the dark season, and the vital juices retire. Nature spreads its final charm; even as it is dying away, it still gives us its splendor one last time: Everything becomes colorful, and fog wraps nature in a milky light, dewdrops glitter between cobwebs, berries shine, and mushrooms sprout.

There are some themes of the celebration: Harmony and balance; giving thanks for the harvest; thinking about the previous year; preparation for the time to come.

Ask yourself: What am I grateful for? What has taken on balance? What do I still have to work on? What was good? What could have gone better? What has accompanied me?

Master

How do I prepare myself for the dark time ahead? Attune yourself to the quality of this specific time. Choose your cards and then begin laying them out.

Card Divination Pattern:
Base (Elemental power)
    1. Which natural force accompanies me? Which message do I receive from nature?
General (Foundation)
    2. What was the quintessence of recent times?
    3. Central theme: Thanksgiving

Joker

    4. What am I grateful for?
    5. What do I still have to work on?
    6. What has the year brought to me?
    7. What needs to be observed for the upcoming time?

Companion (Support)
8. Which force is accompanying me now?

Master (Apprenticeship)
9. Under which star does the upcoming time stand?

Joker (Surprise)
10. Which force is helping and supporting me at this moment?

Here are some special questions in case a ritual is supposed to take place:

General/Base
11. What needs to be observed with the Thanksgiving ritual?

General/Companion
12. Which force accompanies our ritual?

General/Master or Joker
13. Which force protects our ritual?

Tip/Advice
If you still wish to explore this theme more deeply, you can work with the Inner and Outer Stages of Change card divination pattern [see p. 136].

General

Ways of the Dragon

Examination

Object of This Card Divination

This card divination pattern can help you to get through examination and testing situations more easily.

Getting into the Right Mood

Base

♥♣♦♠

"Powerful, powerful is the dragon's way. For here, there is no wandering course; here, there is no wriggling and childish play. What counts here, is one's own force, to overcome or to the dragon succumb. Yet if you succeed, you will become one with the dragon's zeal and zest, this strength is forever yours indeed; therefore, embrace this test. Walk the steps of flame, for your strength, it has called your name." (translated from: Im Reich der Naturgeister)

In life, there are many tests. In those exams, we are tested to see if we have truly understood that which we believe to know and whether or not we can apply it. For only then, in its use, can it become a part of our strength.

Here are some questions for attuning yourself: Which exam is coming up for you? On what level does it take place? What can you do in order to prepare yourself for this test?

Companion

Concentrate on it. Observe what is already there for coping with the decisive situation and what you still need. Choose your cards and then begin laying them out.

Card Divination Pattern

Base (Elemental power)

    1. Which elemental power/natural force is supporting me now?

    2. Which elemental power/natural force needs to still be strengthened or needs to be observed in particular?

General (Foundation)

Master

    3. What is the nature of my examination?

    4. What are inhibitory or fostering influences on my path?

With inhibitory influences, you can draw an additional card and pose the question: how can I remedy these inhibitory influences?

    5. The roots: what have I brought with me (my tools, my strength)?

    6. What lies on the way?

    7. What needs to be observed in particular?

    8. What is available to me from within me?

    9. What is available to me from the outside?

Joker

    10. What do I have to let go or leave behind now?

    11. What is helping me?

      (7, 8, 10 are the forces of the past; 6, 9, 11 are the forces of the present.)

    12. What do I still have to work on and what should I still prepare?

    13. What is the possible outcome?

Companion (Support)

14. What accompanies and supports me at this moment?
15. What can I call on if I do not know how to go on?

Master (Apprenticeship)

16. What is the chance, the higher theme of this test?

Joker (Surprise)

17. Unimagined help
18. Trump

Tip/Advice

Concentrate on your exam. Do that which comes easiest to you first because it costs you little strength, and then, after the easy part is out of the way, tackle one by one those aspects that do not come so easy to you. It is important that you do not give up rashly. Activate your resources, reserves, and secret "wonder drug." Go forward and not backward, for your lifetime of happiness lies ahead of you!

General

Three Wishes from the Good Fairy

Gifts from the Cosmos

Object of This Card Divination

Imagine a fairy appears and says to you: "You are granted three wishes." What would you wish for? Three wishes open the gate to other dimensions, to other realms in which miracles are still possible. This card divination pattern serves the recognition of our everyday being and the opening up to the gifts and miracles of the cosmos in everyday life. We all receive gifts from the cosmos daily. Often, we do not see them, as they appear too usual to us; this is because we are not truly present in the here and now, or it may be because we have simply not attuned ourselves to them.

Base

Getting into the Right Mood

Attune yourself to the three wishes of the fairy. Take a few minutes daily and think about what has made you happy today, what has entered your life unexpectedly, what has surprised you, and what has given you a good feeling. What has stimulated you today? What can you be grateful for? What can you praise yourself for? What have you done well? Also think about if you have given someone a little joy today, if you have left a little print of the good force that lies within you with someone in his or her day. Open up to the gifts from the cosmos. Be present, go with open eyes through the day, and begin to discover the everyday, little miracles. Discover the fairy with her magic wand of light along your way, how she smiles at you and tells you: "I am here, do you see? I praise and take joy in thee; three I grant to a child fair. What they are I do not care. But what you wish, consider well; it may come true and what it means you can not tell. It is now in your hands here, with heart, sense, and reason, I thee give; speak it clear and with this live!"

Companion

Card Divination Pattern:

Today the cosmos gives you:

1. A *Joker:* A force that surprises you
2. A *Companion:* A force that accompanies you and protects you
3. A *Master:* A star that shines above you

Master

Joker

In the Realm of Pan
Relation to Animals, Plants, and Minerals

General

Object of This Card Divination
This card divination pattern reveals your relation to nature and to everything that belongs to you.

Getting into the Right Mood
"Spirit of nature, I invoke you! The sylvan valley! Beings of the forest, I invoke you! The fertile valley! Spirit of the land, I invoke you!" (Ritual invocation of nature)

Base

Everything is possessed of a great sense of soul. The number of beings, creatures, and kingdoms that can be found in nature is limitless. We, too, are a part of nature. When we go into nature, we enter the realm of Pan. In here, the oldest realm is that of the stone and mineral kingdom. Then follows the plant kingdom and afterward the animal kingdom. If you wish, you can go into nature to work with this pattern. Look for a quiet place, and listen to the sounds and the noises that surround you. Take in your surroundings with all of your senses. See if there are any animals near you and what kind of plants surround you.

Companion

Here are some questions for attuning yourself: How is your relationship with nature? To which realms and beings do you feel a close connection? Are you conversing with nature? Are you concerned with the preservation of nature? Have you already had contact with the creatures of nature? Choose your cards and then begin laying them out.

Card Divination Pattern
General (Foundation)
1. Central theme: My relation to nature
2. Nature's message to me
3. My relation to stones, minerals, and gemstones
4. The message of the stone kingdom to me

Master

5. My relation to plants
6. The message of the plant kingdom to me
7. My relation to animals
8. The message of the animal kingdom to me
9. My relation to nature and to elemental beings
10. The message of nature spirits to me
11. What is fostering or hindering me in my relation with nature
12. This is what I can do

Base (Elemental power)

Joker

13. This element is accompanying me

Companion (Support)

14. This force accompanies me in nature
15. This force is helping me to take up the connection to nature spirits, animals, plants, and stones

16. This force fosters communication, exchange and understanding
17. This force I can call upon for a sense of earth healing

Master *(Apprenticeship)*

18. The message of creation

Joker *(Surprise)*

19. The medicine
20. The present
21. The healing of the connection between me and nature (the nature spirits, stones, plants, and animals)
22. The force that I can give back to the earth

Tip/Advice

You can modify this card divination pattern by elaborating only on those questions that are currently essential in your

dealing with nature. If, for example, you wish to lay out cards only for animals, you may deal with questions 7, 8, 11, 12, 13, 14, 15, 18, 20, 21, and 22. If, on the other hand, you wish to carry out an earth healing and wish to attempt to come to terms with the other realms at another time, you may lay out cards for questions 1, 2, 9, 10, 11, 12, 13, 14–17, 18, 19, 21, 22.

Be playful in your dealings with nature. If you have a special question, write it down and draw a card for it as well. In this way, you can adapt the card divination pattern to your situation. Seek as often as possible for the paths in nature. Learn to understand their patterns and signs with your heart. They will guide you and lead you.

Assistance from the Elf World
Medicine from Nature

General

Object of This Card Divination
This card divination pattern will help you gain deep realizations about your self and your life.

Getting into the Right Mood

Base

> *"Some things one must first believe before the gate into their worlds opens up,*
> *and one's belief gradually grows into knowledge."*

Elves are the guardians of the plant world. They know and guard the medicine of nature, everything that comes from it and is thus healed. According to the divine spiritual nature (in which the elves are also at home), it is assumed that each illness begins with an imbalance in the divine spiritual level before it reveals itself in the body as pain, illness, or other form of imbalance. For this reason, pain, illness, or imbalance in the body is an indication and a message to us from our soul. It tells us that we had better pay attention to certain aspects of our lives and not to avoid dealing with them.

Companion

Before you begin laying out your cards, close your eyes and concentrate for some time on your body. How does it feel? Where do you experience tension and pain? If you wish, you can pack your cards and a blanket and go into nature: a garden, a forest, or onto a meadow. Be on the lookout for a nice spot where you can spend some time undisturbed. Everywhere there are blooms and growing plants, you know that elves are around. Even though we are not able to see or perceive them most of the time, nevertheless, we can begin, with this consciousness, to open the gates into the realms of nature once more. Choose your cards and then begin laying them out.

Card Divination Pattern

Master

Base (Elemental power)
  1. Which natural force is unbalanced?
  2. Which natural force is supporting me now?

General (Foundation)
  3. Central theme
  4. My body
  5. My spirit
  6. My soul
  7. My feelings

Joker

  8. This is out of balance
  9. This is what needs to be done
  10. The message of the elves

Companion (Support)
  11. This is what accompanies me now

12. This is what supports me in my development

Master (Apprenticeship)

13. This is the superior, cosmic view of my situation

Joker (Surprise)

14. The chance of growth in the situation

15. The medicine and the advice of the elves

Tip/Advice

If you have chosen this card divination pattern, then this is a sure hint that you can find a lot of healing and strength in nature. Go more often out into nature. Look for a spot. There, close your eyes and breathe deeply. Feel your connection with the spot, with nature, and with the beings at this place. Enjoy where you are for a while. With all your being and with all your heart, ask the entities of this place for a sign and for help. Then open your eyes and look around you. What strikes you in particular?

General

Wisdom of the Gnomes

Earth Spirits: Your Talents and Treasures

Object of This Card Divination

This card divination pattern allows inner reflection, connection with the wisdom of the gnomes. Here, you learn about the treasures and talents that lie still hidden within you.

Getting into the Right Mood

Base

"We the old from mountain homes come from the Folk called gnomes. Tarry here a while, my friend. Come wanderer and advice we shall lend. Heed, though: Our words bear a price, payment demanded sometimes thrice. Well, life is after all a wild ride. Thus, inside in yourself take a deeper look, as you will read the message clearly as a book. If you choose to pass, the treasure keep from your mind, for the way was never for you to find. Your problem does not concern us, for we act secretly with none to discern us. Yet, if you take your time and halt now here, you may then see us in our mystery appear. Your cards unpack, your inner gate unlock, and we will call you back. We can take you by the hand and give you messages from the hidden land. Here are the treasures to be mined and the places that help you to find yourself, to see your strengths, and to name them in word and deed. Thus, wealth comes quickly near, for

Companion

your creative power you find here. Let yourself be guided by the hidden means. They lead you safely on inner streams to honor, fame and deserved dreams." (Message of the Gnomes)

When you have attuned yourself, choose your cards and begin laying them out.

Card Divination Pattern

General (Foundation)

  1. This wisdom is in you
  2. This talent I give to you
  3. This realization you can gain
  4. From this you have to refrain
  5. This is the hidden treasure in you
  6. This brings luck and help to you
  7. This brings your wealth to light
  8. Which even matter does not hide

Base (Elemental power)

  9. This natural force stands by your side

Companion (Support)

  10. This companion is here to guide
  11. This companion is to be found here when needed

Master (Apprenticeship)

  12. This message found here is for you

Joker (Surprise)

  13. This is the force that hold the lookout watch for me

14. This is the strength of your true power
15. In this way, you can show your fame

Tip/Advice

It seems very appropriate that you lay this card divination pattern at a spot within nature, for there you are much closer to the realms of nature. In addition, for a deeper or broader insight, you can work with The Element of Earth card divination pattern [see p. 120].

General

A Sign from Salamanders

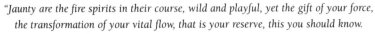
Fire Spirits: The Gift of Your Strength

Object of This Card Divination

With this card divination pattern, you can examine your courage, your strength, your force, and your power more closely.

Getting into the Right Mood

Base

> *"Jaunty are the fire spirits in their course, wild and playful, yet the gift of your force,*
> *the transformation of your vital flow, that is your reserve, this you should know.*
> *Transform the steps of the flame, for the fire has called your name."*

If you have chosen this card divination pattern for yourself, then it is time that you occupy yourself with your inner fire and so listen to the messages of the fire spirits. Take some time for yourself, close your eyes, and listen to your inner flame. Feel your energy, your power, your courage, your warmth, your strength, and your force to change things. You must be willing to transform them and to bring things into the world. Let yourself be guided by these beings of the fire realm. Light a candle for yourself and then begin laying out the cards.

Companion

Card Divination Pattern

Base (Elemental power)
    1. This natural force hinders or fosters my power, my force, my energy
General (Foundation)
    2. Central theme: my wand, my scepter, my force
    3. The base: force/power/strength of my ancestors or my roots
    4. On the one hand: this weakens or this strengthens me
    5. On the other hand: this diminishes or this increases my force
    6. Warning: on this topic I could burn my fingers
    7. Your courage: this needs to be done
    8. Your action: how I am supposed to employ my strength
    9. The change: this should be altered
    10. The advice of the fire spirits: this lets my force become victorious
Companion (Support)
    11. This accompanies me in my force
    12. This helps me to employ my power, my force, and my courage well
Master (Apprenticeship)

Joker

    13. The cosmic fire of my light (for what should I use my force and my power?)
Joker (Surprise)
    14. This transforms my fire and brings it into balance
    15. This I can give to the world through my force
    16. This warns me

Tip/Advice

If you choose this card divination pattern, take a few days to think deeply about your fire and how it translates into your inner force. Take your time in order to grasp the message deep inside of you. In addition, you can work with The Element of Fire card divination pattern [see p. 122].

General

The Mirror of Water Nymphs

Water Spirits: A Glance at Times

Object of This Card Divination

With this mirror, you can glance at past, present, and future situations of life.

Getting into the Right Mood

The magic mirror is guarded by the spirit beings of the water. You should not use this source of wisdom for mere entertainment, but only if you are truly prepared for the message that it sends. The message to be found here corresponds to the hermetic principle and thus reflects your situation of life. Before applying this card divination pattern, close your eyes, and, in your imagination, travel to a body of water: a lake, a river, a pond, the ocean. What form does your inner body of water take? Can you already recognize a hint of a message? Ask yourself whether or not you are really willing to cast a glance into the mirror of your inner depths. If so, attune yourself to the subject in your own manner. Make, for example, a small celebration for yourself out of it. Call upon the beings of water and heaven, in the manner you consider right and honorable, so that they may guide you and stand by your side.

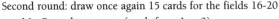
Base

Companion

Card Divination Pattern

General (Foundation)

First round

    1. My spell
    2. My predisposition
    3. My ability, my art
    4. My power
    5. My splendor
    6. My court
    7. The gift of my ancestors
    8. My roots
    9. My belief/my truth
    10. My knowledge
    11. My mind
    12. My skill
    13. My feeling
    14. My profession
    15. My realizations

Master

Second round: draw once again 15 cards for the fields 16-20

    16. Central statement (cards from 1 to 3)
    17. Wanted future (cards from 4 to 6)
    18. Inherited future (cards from 7 to 9)
    19. Envisioned future (cards from 10 to 12)

Joker

20. Lived future (cards from 13 to 15)

Companion (Support)

   21. Accompanying force on the inside

   22. Accompanying force in the outer world

Master (Apprenticeship)

   23. Theme of life

Joker (Surprise)

   24. Helpful twist of fate

   25. The key to my own force

General

In the Realm of Angels
The Bright Forces from the Spiritual World

Object of This Card Divination
This card divination pattern helps you to connect with the realm of angels and to receive the divine messages coming from there.

Getting into the Right Mood

Base

> *"Spiritual worlds, worlds of the mind, send your light down upon me. May the divine word,*
> *the baptism of force descend as a healing experience into my heart. From now on,*
> *I want to be faithful and courageous, a servant of truth." (Flower Newhouse)*

The realms of the angels are always by our side. However, they respect the importance of our free will, and wait until we summon them into our life. The first step to the grounds of spiritual light, where we are able to communicate with these beings of pure light, is to open our heart, indeed, to open ourselves with our entire being. Angelic light is gentle and delicate. It unfolds in our life like a sunrise. The more we train our senses, the better we are in the position to see the grandeur and the light of the light beings.

Companion

Attune yourself in your way to the angels. Prepare yourself to receive their message. Close your eyes for a few minutes. Let your current particulars of life pass in front of your inner eye like a cloud—without assessment, without judgment, simply observing. Where can you see that light is missing? Where can you find beauty and where does it lack? How does it work its effect upon you? Then ask the angels to illuminate your situation and thus bring everything to light. When you have attuned yourself, choose your cards and begin laying them out. In this case, it is recommended to work primarily with several angel card decks.

Card Divination Pattern
Base (Elemental power)
    1. This natural force accompanies me

Master

General (Foundation)
    2. My central theme/my situation of life
    3. This fosters or hinders me in receiving the messages of the angels
    4. This I need to pay attention to
    5. This needs to be done now or left alone in contact with the light realms

Companion (Support)
    6. This force stands by my side
    7. This force leads me into the higher realms
    8. This heavenly force acts through me in this world
    9. This force I can call upon in difficult times or in emergency situations

Joker

Master (Apprenticeship)
    10. The cosmic message of angels for the current life situation

Joker (Surprise)
    11. This is helping me to attain the realm of light

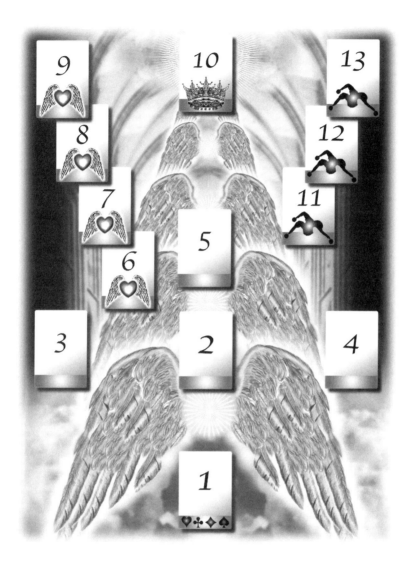

12. The inner key
13. The healing message

Tip/Advice
Try to connect with the bright realms for a longer period of time. Invite the angels to act in your life both in the mornings and the evenings. With time, you will feel their light throughout your life.

General

In the Temple of the Masters
Visit to the Grounds of Light

Object of This Card Divination

This card divination pattern helps you to connect with the grounds of light, to attune yourself to them and to receive the messages from the temple of the masters.

Getting into the Right Mood

Base

The temple of the masters, that great field of energy and focal points of light, has existed at all times. Energy cannot be destroyed but is simply altered from one mode of existence to the next. In this way, all great masters of all times are always present; they send their light upon the earth. Everyone who is ready will receive the light and the wisdom from the temple. With their light, they support us in our development in order to perfect our very own light. Letting our consciousness wander is a wonderful way of traveling. If we open up our consciousness of reality to the areas of light, then we have found within our inner being the ways and means to travel on the wings of our thoughts and spiritual power to the temple of the masters. We are able to absorb the strength, the beauty, the wisdom, the love, the compassion, the understanding, the force, and peace . . . everything that we find there in order to implement this experience in our world and our daily life. Attune yourself to the grounds of the masters' light. How do they reveal themselves in your imagination? What can you experience there for yourself? Let your thoughts rest for some time in these realms. When you feel ready, choose your cards and begin laying them out.

Companion

Card Divination Pattern

Base (Elemental power)
  1. Which natural force is acting at this moment?

General (Foundation)
  2. How is my relation to the grounds of light of the masters?
  3. What are the hindering or fostering influences going along with it?
  4. What needs to be done or left alone in order for me to get in touch with this force?
  5. What can I learn/experience now?

Companion (Support)
  6. Which force accompanies me to the grounds of light?
  7. Which force is helping me to increase my energy?

Master (Apprenticeship)
  8. What does the message of the realms of light state?

Joker (Surprise)
  9. What is the gift of the realms of light?
  10. What medicine do I receive for my healing?
  11. What is the task for the upcoming time?

Master

Joker

Tip/Advice

Work with the masters for some time. In order to set the stage for growth, before going to bed, prepare yourself for a journey to the temple of a master who is important for you. Cleanse yourself and come to terms with your workday before going to bed, so that this journey is not done while sleeping. What did the day give you? What gave you joy? What occupied you? Allow a candle to burn for some time. Let the workday stream out of your body with each exhalation, and let the light stream into your body with each inhalation. Ask your master or masters for guidance and instruction.

General

Footsteps of the Gods and Goddesses
Encounter with Your Force and Your Power

Object of This Card Divination

To follow the footsteps of the gods and goddesses means to follow the traces the force and power only to discover them inside one's own person.

Getting into the Right Mood

> *"The one God has no face and at the same time infinitely many."*

Base

Walking in the footsteps of the gods and goddesses allows for the activation of greater forces so that what was once dim now shines in the darkness. How this happens is perhaps best described by what I experienced on my Shamanic journey:

I reached the heaven of the the gods and goddesses. I saw them all. Some were strong and shining and their mighty light filled and nourished the earth. Others, on the other hand, were sma0ll, insignificant, and appeared stunted. Their light shone only dimly. I observed this spectacle in the heaven of the gods for some time, and all of a sudden my glance fell upon the earth. I saw the energy threads that spun between the human beings and the gods and goddesses. The brightly shining gods and goddesses that were mighty and full of energy and nourished our planet with their forceful light had many followers who

Companion

remembered them, called upon them, rendered homage to them, and worshipped them; in this way, these disciples provided them with power. They radiated the light sent to them by us back upon all of us by a thousandfold. Those gods and goddesses, on the other hand, who were small and stunted had completely fallen into oblivion on earth, or, at best, there were only a few people who remembered them. In this way, I understood that that which we send out will be reflected within the cosmos in a manifold manner and then returned to us in a much greater context.

Here are some questions for attuning yourself: Which gods and goddesses have you

Master

encountered in your life? What do they embody for you? Which part of your personality or your life do they illuminate? Which force can you activate with this part? Which divine aspects are supposed to regain their firm place in your life? Which divine force would you like to awaken in you? Which "divine track" would you like to follow within you?

Card Divination Pattern

Base (Elemental power)

   1. This natural force acts in my life particularly strongly

General (Foundation)

Joker

   2. Central theme

   3. This force needs to be activated or diminished in my life

   4. The track of the gods and goddesses in my life

   5. The sacrifice to the gods and goddesses

   6. Access to the upper spheres

Companion (Support)

7. This force accompanies me into the heaven of the goddesses and gods

8. This force acts through me

Master (Apprenticeship)

9. The message of the goddesses and gods for me

Joker (Surprise)

10. The healing drink

11. The divine strength that I can develop now

12. The gift of the goddesses and the gods

Tip/Advice

Dwell for some time upon the innumerable faces of the divine, with all of its aspects and reflections. With time, you will discover the divine in everything; the usual tendency to think in terms of "either" and "or" will dissolve into "as well as."

The Principle of Spirituality

General

Object of This Card Divination

The principle of spirituality can be of assistance for meditation and realization in order to understand the great forces in the universe and to transfer them to our personal life.

Getting into the Right Mood

Theme: The principle of spirituality: One is everything; everything one. All is spiritual; there is nothing apart from spirit. The outer world and the universe are spiritual.

Base

Significance: With this principle, it is all about explaining the nature of the substance from which everything is created. "Everything is spiritual" means that all material, emotional, mental and other forms of appearance are in the end spiritual energies in various forms of expression. Energy is mutable. The person who understands the spiritual nature of the universe has progressed far on the way to mastery.

We see nothing but the transformation of spiritual energy, the true natural state on all levels when we observe the outer world and the universe of which we are a part. The only consistent thing is the change. If we wish to use the principle of spirituality within our own lives, then this means that we are a part of the whole, we are in eternal change, and we are

Companion

nothing but energy. With this energy, we are able to change ourselves and others in one or the other direction. Attune yourself to the principle of spirituality. Concentrate on your question or your problem, and try to see it with the perspective of spirituality. Which delicate energy do you feel behind your question, theme, or problem? Meditate and concentrate on your thoughts for five to ten minutes: Remember that everything is spiritual. "There is nothing apart from spirit." What does this mean to you in relation to your question, theme, or problem? In which context does it relate to the great whole? When you have attuned yourself, choose your cards and then begin laying them out.

Master

Card Divination Pattern

General (Foundation)

    1. Central theme: What is the question/problem?

    2. Which energy stands behind it?

    3. What is the cause on a higher level?

    4. What is my task at this point?

    5. What are the consequences on a higher level if I take on the task?

    6. What happens or changes in my life then?

Companion (Support)

    7. Which force accompanies me?

Master (Apprenticeship)

Joker

    8. Under which star does my question, theme, or problem stand?

Joker (Surprise)

    9. At this moment, what is helping me to transform my energy?

The Principle of Correspondence

General

Object of This Card Divination

With this principle of correspondence you can examine how things stand in relation to one another. It serves to illuminate the theme you raise more brightly, and, by doing so, we can come to understand it and arrive at any number of possibilities: resolution, change, transformation, dissolution, or even re-creation.

Getting into the Right Mood

Base

Theme: As it is on the top, so it is on the bottom. As it is on the inside thus it is on the outside. Microcosm equals macrocosm.

Significance: The principle of correspondence makes it possible for the human being to draw conclusions from the known to the unknown, from the small to the big and vice versa. This means, for example, that a person can come to understand the themes of life of another person, who is born under a certain constellation, simply by observing the position of the stars.

There are many levels of experience beyond our knowledge, yet if we apply the principle of correspondence, we can come to understand concepts that we would otherwise not be able to grasp. In our own lives, we can only experience that which strikes a certain resonance within us; thus this is what finds a certain correspondence within us. In this way, when we experience something, we can come to recognize where its particular correspondence lies within us. When we bring forth this correspondence and begin to change from that point, the transformation will also show on the outside. As the principle promises, if we change the outside, the inside changes; if the inside changes, so the outside will change; if we change big things, small things change, and if we change small things, big things will change. Everything stands in sympathetic relation with everything, for the universe is all spirit.

Companion

When you have a problem or when an idea occupies you a great deal, then try to put this problem or theme into words as precisely as possible. Ask yourself: What might be deep inside of me that causes me to raise this theme or problem? What have I not solved or not looked at deep within me? Exactly where inside me does the topic find its perfect resonance? At which places in my life has this theme previously appeared? When you have chosen your card deck(s), begin laying them out.

Master

Card Divination Pattern

General (Foundation)

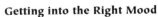
Joker

1. The theme/the problem
2. What am I supposed to learn from it?
3. What is inside of me?
4. What comes from the outside?
5. How do I see it?

6. How do others see it?
7. Where is there a correspondence or resonance within me?
8. What do I have to resolve or work on so that there is no longer a correspondence in me?

Companion (*Support*)

9. Which force accompanies and supports me?

Master (Support)

10. Under which star does this correspondence stand?

Joker (*Surprise*)

11. What helps me to resolve this old pattern?
12. What is healing me?

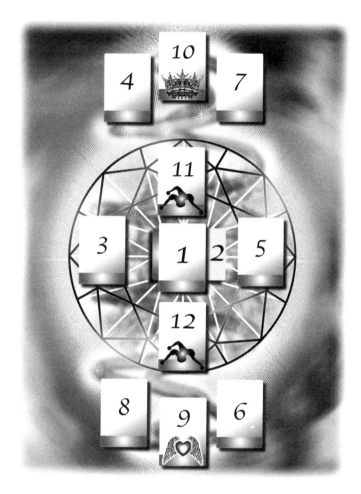

Tip/Advice

If you work with this pattern, please be aware that coincidence is that which is supposed to accidentally encounter you, which correlates with your current situation. If you change your inner picture, the outer must change as well, according to the universal law of correspondence.

The Principle of Vibration

General

Object of This Card Divination

With the principle of vibration, you can ascertain how events or ideas stand in relation to one another. This spread serves to examine a question, a theme, or a problem more thoroughly, in order to understand it for any number of possibilities: alteration, transformation, or even re-creation. In addition to this, the spread can also serve as a meditative aid.

Getting into the Right Mood

Base

Theme: Nothing is truly in complete silence. Everything is constantly in motion, and so everything vibrates.

Significance: Everything is in motion, from the lightest to the firmest state. Everything vibrates, nothing is in quietude. The faster the vibration, the higher the state or level. Through the various degrees of vibration, various states of energy arise. The vibration of the spirit, for example, has such a high frequency that it actually almost returns to a sense of quiet. The slower the object or idea oscillates, the more idle the substance. We can, though, elevate the vibration with our spiritual energy; we can build people up with it, stimulate them, inspire them, and heal them. On the other hand, with a low vibration, we can pull people down in our environment, making them sick, and even keep ourselves in a low vibrating state, thus exacerbating the problem. When we understand this principle, then we hold in our hands the key to our personal power.

Companion

Here are some questions for attuning yourself: How high or low do I assess my vibration? How much energy do I have? What kind of effect do I have on my environment? What gets me into a higher state of vibration? What elevates my vibration? What pulls it down? What sort of quality does my question, problem, or theme have? What about it drags me down? What do I have to change? Attune yourself to this principle and then begin laying out your cards.

Master

Card Divination Pattern

General (Foundation)

    1. Central theme: The question or the problem

    2. Which quality does your theme have?

    3. What elevates the quality?

    4. What diminishes the quality?

    5. What helps to positively transform the energy?

    6. What needs to be done or left alone?

Joker

    7. What enters into the world through this?

Companion (Support)

    8. Which force helps to increase the vibration?

Master (Apprenticeship)

    9. Under which star does this development stand?

Joker (Surprise)

    10. What is helping and healing me now?

The Principle of Polarity

Object of This Card Divination

With the principle of polarity, a means has been given to you to observe a question, theme, or problem from various points of view and to possibly alter, change, and understand both your point of view and the problem by doing so. In addition, this card divination pattern can also serve as a meditative aid.

Getting into the Right Mood

Base

Theme: Everything has two poles. Everything has two sides that belong to the same single entity. Everything has its pair of opposites. Equal and unequal are actually the same. Opposites are identical.

Significance: A coin has a front and a back side, yet it is still one and the same coin. Each thing has two sides. The principle at hand explains that there are two poles in everything, or opposite aspects. We need to come to recognize that opposites are only parts of the one thing, diverging only in extremes or degrees. Some of our most common pairs of opposites are light/dark, hot/cold, day/night. Love and hate stem from one and the same energy. Every one of us knows, in one way or another, how truly close together these emotional states really lie. How quickly can love be turned into hatred and

Companion

hatred into love or, if expressed in a different intensity, how quickly can affection turn into aversion and the other way around. Through this principle, a master is able to alter conditions by force of will and turn them to the better. We can even recognize the light through the dark force.

Here are some questions for attuning yourself: Which theme is currently occupying you? What do the two poles of the topic look like? Toward which pole are you leaning and what must this tendency inevitably trigger with the other one? Attune yourself to the principle, and then begin laying out your cards.

Master

Card Divination Pattern

General (Foundation)

1. Central theme: The question/the problem
2. The one pole of the theme
3. The other pole of the theme
4. This needs to be done so that I achieve balance or that I can recognize the whole picture
5. Observed from one pole (from one's own perception)
6. Observed from the other pole (from the opposite perspective)
7. This I need to be doing right now

Companion (Support)

Joker

8. This force helps me to find balance and the right measure of action

Master (Apprenticeship)

9. Under this star does this development stand

Joker *(Surprise)*

    10. This is helping me now to recognize the two sides of an affair and to turn what is wrong to the better

Tip/Advice

If you wish to illuminate a topic even more brightly, you should try to recognize within any subject its opposite. With the strength of your will, you will be able to bring the poles into balance and to change their opposition into something good.

The Principle of Rhythm

General

Object of This Card Divination

With the principle of rhythm, you can examine how things are standing in relation to one another. This card divination pattern serves to look at a question, a theme, or a problem more thoroughly. By doing so, it serves to bring us to a sense of understanding, possibly in order to change it or to reshape the issue through this greater understanding. In addition, this spread can act as a meditative assistance.

Getting into the Right Mood

Base

Theme: Every thing has its time, rising and falling. There is a rhythm within everything.

Significance: Everything flows in and out, and all things have their time and rhythm. To the extent in which something streams in, it must also stream out once more. Low tide and high tide, inhaling and exhaling . . . there is always action and therefore, as we know, there must be a reaction that consequently becomes a new action which then triggers once again a reaction. This principle is revealed in everything that is: from the rise and fall of ages and of civilizations to a person being born and dying.

Through the work with this principle, you can learn to understand the rhythm of life in such a way as to make use of it for yourself. For example, when you feel that you are completely

Companion

down, take comfort knowing that life must rise again at one point. If you have been very active, then quietude is beckoning you. The farther you draw back and aim the arrow back on your inner bow, the faster and more precisely it hits its goal when you release it. The more conscientiously you prepare yourself on the inside, the better will be the result on the outside. With this principle you have the opportunity to balance out the conditions in your life.

Ask yourself: To which rhythm do I surrender myself? What has recently been the movement within me? Which movements, therefore, must necessarily follow? Have I been active and this is why I am, therefore, withdrawing right now? Or was I withdrawn and thus am striving toward the outside once more? Which movement is currently taking place in

Master

nature; does it retreat or does it emerge? Do I live the various rhythms in me consciously? What is now in store for me?

Concentrate on the topic and feel the beneficial force of the rhythm between the poles. Then begin laying out your cards.

Card Divination Pattern

General (Foundation)

Joker

1. Central theme: The question or the problem
2. What lies hidden behind this topic?
3. Which movement have I experienced during recent times?
4. Which movement must follow now?
5. What needs to be done?
6. What shall rest?
7. What is next on the agenda for me?

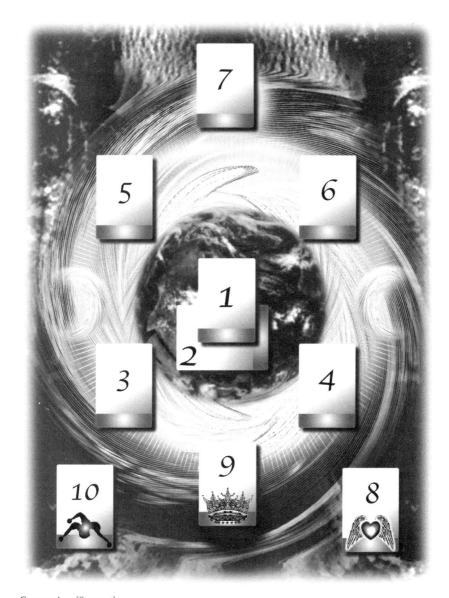

Companion (*Support*)

    8. Which force accompanies me and helps me to find the rhythm?

Master (*Apprenticeship*)

    9. Under which star does the current time stand?

Joker (*Surprise*)

    10. What is supporting me at this moment?

General

The Principle of Cause and Effect

Object of This Card Divination

With the principle of cause and effect, you can examine how things are developing as one thing emerges from the other. The card divination pattern serves to examine a question, theme, or problem more thoroughly, to understand it and by doing so, afford the opportunity to alter it, to transform it, or to create it anew. In addition, working with this spread can serve as a meditative aid.

Base

Getting into the Right Mood

Theme: As a man sows, so shall he reap. Each cause has an effect and each effect has a cause.

Significance: This principle says that everything happens according to a set pattern. Nothing is accidental. Anything that is sent out returns in form to the sender. Of course, there are various levels of cause and effect. The higher levels dominate the lower levels. However, nothing can escape this principle. A master raises himself to a higher level so that he becomes the cause and yet is able to recognize the effect.

Here are some questions for attuning yourself: What seeds have you already sown today, in thoughts, words, feelings, or action? What grows in your inner garden? What kind of energy have you sent out? What can return in terms of energy with what you have sent out? What have you already harvested in your life but did not recognize as harvest?

Companion

Attune yourself to the theme and then begin laying out the cards.

Card Divination Pattern

General (Foundation)

For points 1 through 4, draw two cards: one for that what you have sown; one for what you have harvested. Now, draw an additional card for points 1 through 4 in order to reveal what has played a role in the hidden.

Master

1. That which I have sown so far/That which I have harvested up to this point/That has played a hidden role—on an energetic or ethereal level (energy)
2. On a mental level (thoughts)
3. On an emotional level (feelings)
4. On a material level (matter, action)
5. What can I yet sow?
6. What is helping me?

Companion (Support)

7. What accompanies me and supports me in my inner growth?

Joker

Master (Apprenticeship)

8. Under which energy does my current process of growth stand?

Joker (Surprise)

9. Which force is currently helping my healing?

If there were dark cards on top of the levels, then, for each dark card (that is, for each unsettled card), you may draw a joker with the question: How is the card in question to be healed?

Tip/Advice

Be cognizant in the upcoming time of what you are sending out. Perceive how it feels and what subsequently comes of it. Is it healing or rather debilitating? Learn to move from recognizing effects to recognizing the cause.

The Principle of Gender

General

Object of This Card Divination

With the principle of gender, you can examine how things are standing in relation to one another. This card divination pattern allows us to look at a question, theme, or problem more thoroughly in order to understand it, and thus to possibly alter it, transform it, or even to create it anew. In addition, this spread can serve as a meditative aid.

Getting into the Right Mood

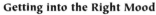

Base

Theme: Gender is in everything. Everything has masculine and feminine sides. There are masculine sides within the feminine, and there are feminine sides within the masculine. Gender reveals itself on all levels.

Significance: The masculine and feminine principle is always at work in creation. In fact, no creation is possible without the complementary presence of this principle. In higher spheres, moreover, it takes on higher forms. Independent of whether we are in this world as a man or as a woman, both sides of the principle work in us—the active male and the receptive female one. Under the auspices of the female side falls the dark, the warm, the nurturing, the receiving, the awaiting, and the invisible. Under the identity of the male side falls the light, the cold, the active, the protecting, the visible. If we think deeply upon this principle, we can bring the forces captured in it into balance within us.

Companion

Here are some questions for attuning yourself: How does my feminine side feel in regards to the theme or the question? How does my masculine side feel? In what ways do these two sides harmonize within me regarding the theme or the question? Does one side become overemphasized? Where does the balance lie; what must be balanced so that something beneficial can result from it? Attune yourself to the principle and then begin laying out your cards.

Master

Card Divination Pattern

General (Foundation)/*Base* (Elemental power)

1. Central theme: The question or the problem
2. The masculine side
3. This needs to be observed with the masculine side
4. This lies hidden within my masculine side
5. In this way my masculine side shows itself on the outside
6. The feminine side
7. This needs to be observed with the feminine side
8. This lies hidden within my feminine side
9. In this way my feminine side shows itself on the outside
10. How do my masculine and feminine sides stand to one another
11. In this way, I can bring the feminine side into balance
12. In this way, I can bring the masculine side into balance

Joker

Companion *(Support)*

13. + 14. This accompanies me in my feminine and in my masculine forces

Master *(Apprenticeship)*

   15. Under this star do these forces stand

Joker *(Surprise)*

   16. This in my feminine force helps me and heals me

   17. This in my masculine force helps me and heals me

Twelve Houses

Object of This Card Divination

With the help of this is card divination pattern you can have a look at the quality of a new year's cycle. It is, therefore, especially suitable at the beginning of a new year, e.g., New Year's Eve, Samhain, or on one's birthday, just to name a few. Here, you can observe via a particular theme what awaits you in the upcoming new year cycle. Moreover, the Twelve Houses can also be used at any time to take a kind of inner inventory to aid in a reflection on your life's themes.

Base

Getting into the Right Mood

A year consists of twelve months, known as the Houses. The Houses cover the greatest collection of themes that occupy us human beings. Take an inventory in regards to how the previous year passed for you. You may either just think about it or take some brief notes. By doing so, you can orient yourself toward the themes of the respective Houses.

Here are some questions for attuning yourself: During the past year, how was your general mood? What was the general state of your belongings? What details did you perceive? After letting the previous year's cycle pass by you once more, you should then attune yourself afterward to the upcoming new year of life, to the new cycle that lies ahead of you. What are your wishes in various areas of life? What are your concerns? What is next on the agenda? What are your goals? Take the card decks (up to four are possible) that you would like to work with, and then begin by laying out your cards.

Companion

Card Divination Pattern

General (Foundation)

> Draw for each point three cards.
> The first round of cards refers to the question: What am I taking with me from the old year? (Past)
> The second round of cards refers to the question: What helps or hinders me? (Present)
> The third round of cards refers to the question: What is the carrying force in the new circle of the year? (Future)

Master

1. This is how I am—General mood/starting point
2. My possession—Security/Finances/property
3. My experiences—Everyday life/basic themes/little journeys
4. My home—Roots/family/safety
5. My expression—Creativity/fun/games
6. My order—Tasks/work/profession
7. My inner balance—Partnership/love/the union of love
8. My depths—Hidden or enigmatic things/shadow sides/crisis/secret power

Joker

9. My possibilities—Higher realizations/great journeys/expanding one's horizon
10. My work—Recognition/professional future/successes
11. My community spirit—Experiences in society and in groups/friendships/team
12. My ideals—secret hopes, anxieties/yearnings/fears

Companion (Support)
13. That which guides me

Master (Apprenticeship)
14. Under this star the year stands

Joker (Surprise)
15. The key

Tip/Advice

For additional insight, you can work with the Wheel of the Year card divination pattern [see p. 182].

Steps of Inauguration

General

Object of This Card Divination

You can use this card divination pattern when you have the feeling that you are standing before a step to a higher level or an inaugural step in life. You may also use this if you wish to explore an overall theme of inauguration.

Getting into the Right Mood

Base

The inauguration (= initiation, from Latin, means an introduction or leading into some-thing) is a gradual introduction into the mysteries of life. Such an initiation can last for a lifetime or for an infinite number of lives. How long depends on us, our willingness for self-development, and on how we use our strength and power within our sense of free will.

There were and are many secret societies and mystery cabals that have their own reg-ulations, rites, and inauguration ceremonies. Yet life itself leads us through the mysteries of life by way of the steps of inauguration. Several of the great steps within a life are birth, the transition from child to adult, parenthood, developing a professional life, independence, and finally death. In between there are an infinite number of steps. Each section of life, each form of new energy, each fright, all the pain, each illness, all the journeys—any and all of

Companion

these can represent an inauguration.

Even if we expose ourselves to certain situations in ritual fashions (e.g., sun dance, seeking of vision, fasting), these still represent a kind of inauguration. Inaugurations always take place when energy changes in such a way that nothing is as it once was. If you have the feeling that you are standing in front of such a portal, then ask yourself: Have I prepared myself for this? What kind of gate is this that I am facing right now? What is changing for me? Which forces are available to me? What is helping me to walk through this gate? What reserves can I call upon? What strengths do I carry inside of me? As soon as you have attuned yourself, choose your cards and then begin laying them out.

Master

Card Divination Pattern

Base (Elemental power)

    1. Which natural force is fostering or hindering me now?

General (Foundation)

    2. What is the threshold or the gate of this inauguration?

    3. What is the guardian or custodian of the threshold? (Here, it is all about the characteristic that needs to be acquired or overcome so that the gate opens for the inauguration. If you have the feeling that you do not possess or that you are not able to overcome this characteristic, then the drawing of the cards should come to an end at this point for right now. Draw only one companion with the ques-tion: What force can help me to acquire this feature?)

Joker

    4. Which direction does it take? What serves as a signpost? What gives helpful impulses?

5. What strengthens your willpower, your endurance, and your perseverance?
6. What do I need for the examination, what proper knowledge, and which kind of skillfulness?
7. What is important in this respect; what is the significant reflection?
8. What is initiating me into the element of air? What is the realization?
9. What is initiating me into the element of water? What is my connection to it? What is illusion and what is reality?
10. What is initiating me into the element of earth? Where do I find inner collection?

11. What is initiating me into the element of fire? What is the sacrifice or the gift?
12. What is initiating me into the element of ether? What is the task or the purpose?
13. The outcome

Companion *(Support)*

14. Who is the guide or the companion by my side?
15. Who is the teacher or the examining force?

Master *(Apprenticeship)*

16. What is the new energy or the blessing of this inauguration?

Joker *(Surprise)*

17. What is the emergency reserve? What helps me if I do not know how to go on?
18. What is my silent reserve?
19. Which force have I won? What am I able to bring into the world now?

Ritual

General

Object of This Card Divination
If you wish to perform a ritual, you can observe with this card divination pattern what the signs mean regarding it, and what needs to be done to observe it properly.

Getting into the Right Mood

Base

> *"Rituals are matters of an individual or of an entire community. They are born out of life, grant life, inform us, and flow back into life. They are magic and religious acts with the purpose of securing harmony between beings and things, human beings and the divine-spiritual, as well as visible and invisible forces. In this way, deep connections become visible and clearly known to us." (Björn Ulbrich)*

A ritual is a self-created free space in which the forces of the cosmos, the forces of the earth, and the currently working forces link, reveal themselves, and are able to dance with one another. A ritual serves to create a connection between the visible and the invisible; furthermore, it serves to create a space in which the connection of all forces is strengthened and where an exchange can take place. A ritual serves to honor forces, to recognize them, to communicate with them, to conjure them up, to call upon them so that they can take effect in one's own life and in the life of the community. The ritual word should always contain a bit more than it obviously seems to express.

Companion

A ritual orients itself by observing the following points: There is always a holy center, acting as a center point. The four forces of the four directions are announced, and a connection is created between the visible and invisible participants. There is an initiation ceremony, a core ritualistic action, a concluding rite, and the ritual meal in which all participants share food and drink. A ritual should remind one of a wavy encircling line. The action increases, rises until its climax, and then declines once again until it reaches its initial energy.

Master

Before you begin with a ritual, ask yourself: What is my intention? What connections do I wish to strengthen? Which forces do I wish to call upon? Which elements and magical actions are important in the ritual (e.g., singing, writing poetry, dancing, meditating)? In which way is protection granted? What needs to be observed? What course is the ritual supposed to take? What do I need for the ritual? What is needed in terms of preparation? How can I be assured that I am not disturbed as I am performing the ritual? If you prepare your ritual and have planned it well, then choose your cards and begin laying them out.

Card Divination Pattern

Joker

Base (Elemental power)
   1. Which natural force needs to be observed?
General (Foundation)
   2. What is the central theme of the ritual?
   3. What is the center?

4. Which signs must by all means be observed?
5. What is the visible force?
6. What is the invisible force?
7. Who are the invited participants?
8. Who are the uninvited participants?
9. What needs to be thought of and taken into consideration?
10. What can I do?
11. What is the essence of the ritual?

Companion (Support)

12. Which force accompanies and protects this ritual?
13. Which force can I call upon in difficult situations that might possibly occur during the ritual?
14. Which force supports the ritual leader and acts through him/her?

Master (Apprenticeship)

15. Under which star does this ritual stand?

Joker (Surprise)

16. What is helpful?
17. What is healing?
18. Which force is being awoken/called/strengthened?

Tip/Advice

In order to further strengthen this theme, you may continue working with the card divination patterns in the Hermetic Principles chapter [see. pp. 256–269].

Inner and Outer Journeys

Object of This Card Divination

With this card divination pattern, you have the opportunity to examine your inner and outer journeys more closely.

Getting into the Right Mood

Base

"You know when the journey begins." (Luisa Francia)
"Traveling means to change the world around you
and to immerse life in a new fame."

When we go on a journey, there are many reasons to do so. Perhaps we wish to become familiar with an area we have only heard about. Or we may wish to see someone or something once again. Or we may wish to escape the routine of our everyday life, or wish to experience something; we may want to broaden our horizon and thus to open ourselves once again to the moment of life. Or we may wish to expand the depth, the width, and the length of our existence. Perhaps we also want to flee merely in order to find ourselves.

Though there are many kinds of journeys, they can be divided in two essential categories: outer and inner. We are also able to travel spiritually to any place in the world and subsequently learn new things about us and our own life. Each journey, no matter how short it might be, will bring a change with it.

Companion

Here are some questions for attuning yourself: What journeys have you already experienced? What have you learned on these journeys? Which experiences remained stuck in your mind? Were there journeys that changed your life forever? What realizations have you won on journeys? Have you ever consciously traveled on the inside? Allow your journeys to pass mentally and observe them. Then attune yourself to the journey that lies ahead of you. Is it an inner or an outer journey? What is the order, the task, the goal of this journey? Do you undertake it for yourself or for someone else? What does your gut feeling tell you in regards to this journey? Does the thought trigger joy or depression? Do you feel prepared for this journey? Take a few moments and concentrate on the journey that lies ahead of you. Listen to your thoughts and feelings, perhaps most importantly to your inner voice. Then choose your cards and begin laying them out.

Master

Card Divination Pattern

Base (Elemental power)

    1. Which natural force acts on my journey?

General (Foundation)

Joker

    2. What is the central theme of the journey?
    3. How are the signs (favorable/not-so-favorable)?
    4. What is the outer reason for this journey?
    5. What is the inner reason for this journey?
    6. What should be considered beforehand?

7. What worries me?
8. What do I expect from this, and what do I hope for?
9. What lies on the path?
10. Which signs do I need to observe during the journey?
11. What is the actual calling?

Companion (*Support*)

12. What accompanies me on my journey?
13. Which force can I call upon in ambiguous situations?
14. Which force reveals itself to me on my journey?

Master (*Apprenticeship*)

15. Under which star does my journey stand?

Joker (*Surprise*)

16. What else is available to me?
17. What protects me?
18. What is the chance of growth?

Realization—Illumination

General

Object of This Card Divination
This card divination pattern can serve as an aid for realization and meditation.

Getting into the Right Mood
There are many moments in life when we find ourselves asking: What is it all for? What is the sense of life? Is there any at all? What am I doing here? What is my destination? This card divination pattern helps you in your to attempt to come to terms with the elementary questions of life. Before you begin laying out your cards, attune yourself to the silence and quietude within you. Breathe deeply, and allow your thoughts and feelings to pass by you like the clouds in the sky. Simply observe them. If you are confident that your attention is in the here and now, begin with the laying out of your cards.

Base

Card Divination Pattern
Base (Elemental power)
    1. Which natural force needs my attention now?
General (Foundation)
    2. Who am I?
    3. What is the sense or the calling of my life?
    4. Where do I come from?
    5. To where does my calling lead me?
    6. What is my task of life/my theme of life?
    7. What can be redeemed through this?
Companion (Support)
    8. What accompanies me from the spiritual world?
    9. Which energy supports me in all situations of life?
    10. Which force acts through me in this world?
Master (Apprenticeship)
    11. What is the superior sense/the higher task of my life?
Joker (Surprise)
    12. The help within me
    13. The healing on my way
    14. The chance of growth in this life

Companion

Master

Joker

Ancient Oath

Obstacles to One's Luck: Ancient Oaths, Spells, Curses

General

Object of This Card Divination

This card divination pattern helps you to recognize those things in your life that can hinder you from discovering your luck. These things—which can include a curse, a spell, or an oath—exist within one's subconscious, can stem from childhood experiences, or could have been brought along from an earlier life.

Base

Getting into the Right Mood

There are happenings, behavioral patterns, and themes in one's life that defy any kind of reason and logic. We can try to do as much as we want about them, we can even seek professional advice, yet they simply do not resolve themselves; they may even take on a disturbingly active role in our lives, jumping at us without warning as from an ambush. If such a phenomenon exists, then this certainly has to do with something that has its origin in the realms of the soul, energy, or spirit. In order to not merely scratch the surface of the difficulty, it is important to return to the origin of the problem, to find the actual trigger, and thus untie the knot. Then the symptom will slowly dissolve, as it no longer has any kind of base from which to disturb your peace.

Companion

Many of us do not believe in rebirth and in the possibility of an earlier life. Yet even someone who does not believe can have an inner picture of how one's deepest inner being can imaginatively emerge in order to redeem and change the embodied theme so encountered, and thus, through resolution, dissolve the matter. Terms such as "curse," "spell," "bond," and "oath" help us to cope with the feelings that come up by concocting a term with which we can work better. Whatever rises from the depth in pictures and images, however so absurd they may appear to our reason, needs space in order to take effect. In this way, the difficulty can be recognized, lived once again, and then can be forgiven and dissolved.

Master

Before you begin with the laying of your cards, call your request once more to your mind. What is the theme that you are continually confronted with in your life? What was your greatest nightmare during your childhood? What runs like a central thread through your life? What do you experience again and again in your life in various modifications? Take your time and concentrate on what is repeatedly knocking on your door as a life theme. Try to formulate the theme with a concise catchphrase, a headline, or a sentence. What adage or conviction stands behind it? Create a space for this theme in which you can engage it consciously. The more intensely you attempt to come to terms with it, the clearer the messages of the cards become for you. As soon as you have attuned yourself to the theme, choose your cards and then begin laying them out.

Joker

Card Divination Pattern

Base (Elemental power)
1. Which natural force is acting here?
2. To which elemental realm am I supposed to give particular attention?

General (Foundation)

3. What is the central theme? What is it all about?
4. What is the hidden side of the theme?
5. What stands in connection with the theme?
6. What is the root or the cause of the theme?
7. What derives from the line of ancestors?
8. What rises up from the depth?
9. What kind of memory accompanies me?
10. Which feeling do I have?
11. What was the key experience?
12. What is to be done now?

Companion (Support)

13. Which force is supporting me right now?
14. Which force is helping me to come to terms with this theme?

Master (Apprenticeship)

15. What does the cosmos say about this?

Joker (Surprise)

16. What has not been taken into consideration yet?
17. What helps to resolve the old issue?
18. Which medicine is healing me?

Tip/Advice

Take a longer period of time than usual for this theme. Let the cards rest for some time and allow them to have an effect. Look at them repeatedly at certain intervals. Ask for the key to realization and resolution. Pay attention to your feelings and especially your dreams within the next three days, for these are messages that come to you within your everyday life. A theme that has been announcing itself over and over again for so long is worth being heard.

General

Energy Vampire
Loss of Energy and Its Cause

Object of This Card Divination

With this card divination pattern, you can examine possible reasons behind a recent loss of energy.

Getting into the Right Mood

Base

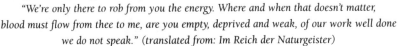
> *"We're only there to rob from you the energy. Where and when that doesn't matter,*
> *blood must flow from thee to me, are you empty, deprived and weak, of our work well done*
> *we do not speak." (translated from: Im Reich der Naturgeister)*

Each of us knows situations in which our energy rapidly declines. We meet certain people and afterward feel tired, exhausted, empty, confused, woozy, and even heavy. We go to bed early, and, even after 13 hours of sleep, we feel absolutely shattered. We often bump into things and inflict small wounds upon ourselves which causes small amounts of blood to flow. If you know such situations then you can be certain that you are dealing with energy vampirism. This process, though, can only take place if you somehow allow it to happen. Some reasons for this can be holes in your energy field stemming from earlier childhood experiences, old patterns, or even predispositions you brought along with you. Or you might have something to hide, a secret to keep.

Companion

Here are some questions for attuning yourself: With what do you surround yourself? When do you feel a clear decline of energy? How does it feel? How are you doing when in contact with people? Which people give you strength? Which ones rob you of your strength? How do you notice that you are losing energy? Which situations and themes trigger this loss of energy? In which situations do you feel a lack within you? On the other hand, when do you feel that you act out of inner strength? When do you act out of a sense of lack? Are you connecting yourself with the divine source? Are you taking care of yourself? What places give you strength? At which places do you feel a clear decline in energy? How do you perceive protection and strength within you? When you have attuned yourself to the theme, then choose your cards and begin laying them out.

Master

Card Divination Pattern

Base (Elemental power)

   1. This natural force needs to be carefully observed in particular

   The element drawn can be a hint as to the area where the energy is extracted from you. Cup/Water = emotional level; Wand/Fire = energetic level; Pentacle/Earth = material level; Sword/Air = mental-spiritual level

General (Foundation)

   2. The vampire

   3. The elixir of life within me

   4. The hidden theme: What it is all about

Joker

5. The gap
6. The bridge
7. That which needs to be observed
8. The healing

Companion (Support)

9. This protects me
10. This is helping me now as I experience a decline of energy

Master (Apprenticeship)

11. This cosmic message is helping me now

Joker (Surprise)

12. This is healing me
13. This helps in tight situations
14. This allows me to build up my protection and my strength

Tip/Advice

If you wish to deepen the theme even further, then you can continue with the Protection and Strength card divination pattern [see p. 284] and with the picture cards in the Hermetic Principles chapter [see pp. 256–269]. Furthermore, you can work with the five elements in order to see where energy abounds and where there is a lack.

Protection and Strength

The Protection Pentagram

General

Object of This Card Divination

If a person cannot protect his or her own person, then the strength is likewise weakened. Conversely, whoever does not feel vigorous becomes unprotected. Strength and protection belong together; freedom comes through strength. This card divination pattern shows how you can come to strength, where your weak points are, what you can work on, and how you can build your protection with it.

Base

Getting into the Right Mood

Take a few minutes for yourself and ponder the themes of protection and strength. How do you feel? Are you full of strength? In which situations do you feel that you are losing your energy? Which situations, on the other hand, give you energy? When do you feel unprotected? When do you feel protected? What do you usually do in order to strengthen yourself? You may wish to take some notes. When you have attuned yourself, choose your cards and begin laying them out.

Companion

Card Divination Pattern

General (Foundation)

    1. Base: The root of my strength

    2. Attitude: What is going on in my head (thoughts, feelings)

    3. Signals: What I am sending to the outside

Companion (Support)

    4. Protection: Who accompanies me

    5. Strength: What weakens or strengthens me

    If a card indicates weakness, draw another one with the question: What can I do in order to remedy this weakness?

Master (Apprenticeship)

    6. Inner sun: What is moving in the center of my strength

Master

Tip/Advice

You can modify this card divination pattern by using a base deck for all points first (e.g., tarot) and by laying out the second round in the above-mentioned sequence but with different decks. In this way, you will gain a deeper insight into the theme. In case there are several hindering forces at work in your protection pentagram, you can then work on your energy system via the card divination patterns in the Health—The Seven Chakras chapter [see pp. 94–109] and especially with the picture card of the Navel Chakra [see p. 100] in order to learn more details about the blockages. In addition, the Energy Vampire card divination pattern [see p, 283] can give you even more detailed information. You may draw an additional card for the negative or blocking forces, or you may examine such a power indi-

Joker

cating card with the Clarifying Ambiguous Cards pattern [see p. 44]. Finally, The Grail Cup card divination pattern [see p. 128] might be helpful in this respect as well.

Visiting the Karmic Council

General

Object of This Card Divination

With the help of this card divination pattern, you can ask the Karmic Council what forces work themselves into you either from this life or from a previous one. From this knowledge, we can determine what needs to be done and resolved. The Karmic Council consists of those angels and masters that guard all records of the movements and functions of all beings.

Base

Getting into the Right Mood

"That which you sow, you will harvest, for today's action determines your tomorrow."
(Zarathustra)

Karma is a word from the Sanskrit, a very old scholarly language from India, and means "acting" or "doing." Karma is the law of cause and effect beyond death; by defining itself in such a way, it embraces the action itself, not the result of this action or some element of destiny. If you wish to examine what "acts," in a Karmic way, ask yourself: What circumstances currently determine my life? Where do the roots for these circumstances lie? Are they a positive force or do they influence me in a negative manner? How can I change

Companion

them? What is now important for me to know? Close your eyes. Concentrate on your question, and ask in your own manner for an answer. Choose your cards and then begin laying them out.

Card Divination Pattern

Base (Elemental power)

    1. This natural force needs to be particularly observed at this moment

Companion (Support)

    2. This force accompanies me to the Karmic Council

Master

General (Foundation)

    3. Deeds from earlier lives

    4. Deeds from the current life

    5. Deeds that have already started to bear fruits

    Decide now into which of the themes from points 3 to 5 you wish to go more deeply.

    6. My inner picture in regards to this theme

    7. Old memories

    8. The former connection (to another human being, a promise, a vow, an oath, an

Joker

       action, a feeling . . .)

    9. What is still having an effect now

    10. What needs to be done

    11. The resulting dissolution, change, or use

    12. The change to which it may come in the future

Companion (Support)

13. The force that supports me in the process

14. The force that stands by my side in difficult situations

Master (Apprenticeship)

15. The cosmic hint of the Karmic Council

Joker (Surprise)

16. The healing medicine

17. The support

18. The key

Tip/Advice

Allow the cards to have an effect upon you for some time. Before going to bed, concentrate once more on the theme. It is advisable to supplicate the cosmic forces and ask them for hints, solutions, and messages. For the next three days be aware of possible hints and messages. You may also continue working with The Karmic Connection card divination pattern [see p. 50].

Index